Mainland China's Taiwan Policy

The Taiwan issue has always been a core national interest of mainland China, which has steadfastly vowed to fulfill national reunification. This book provides a comprehensive and updated explanation of the strategic motivations, behavioral logic, and policymaking rationale of Beijing's Taiwan policy. It will aid readers in predicting the future development of cross-Strait relations, reducing the risk of strategic miscalculations, and defusing potential geostrategic perils.

The book analyzes Beijing's changing policy toward Taiwan during the Kuomintang and Democratic Progressive Party administrations. It explains the key driving forces for Beijing's Taiwan policy in these different periods, which have displayed fundamental shifts from confrontation to cooperation and then back to confrontation. The book also delves into how the rising strategic rivalry between China and the US may influence Beijing's Taiwan policy and the prospect of cross-Strait relations in the near future.

The book will be a useful reference to deepen intellectual understanding of Beijing's broader security and diplomatic policies. It will also appeal to government policymakers who have a keen and vested interest in peace and security in the West Pacific.

Xin Qiang is the inaugural Director of the Center for Taiwan Studies and Deputy Director of the Center for American Studies at Fudan University, China. His research focuses on Taiwan, China–US relations, and maritime security issues.

Routledge Focus on Public Governance in Asia

Series Editors:

Hong Liu, *Nanyang Technological University, Singapore*
Wenxuan Yu, *Xiamen University, China*

Focusing on new governance challenges, practices and experiences in and about a globalizing Asia, particularly East Asia and Southeast Asia, this focus series invites upcoming and established researchers all over the world to succinctly and comprehensively discuss important public administration and policy themes such as government administrative reform, public budgeting reform, government crisis management, public–private partnership, science and technology policy, technology-enabled public service delivery, public health and aging, talent management, and anti-corruption across Asian countries. The book series presents compact and concise content under 50,000 words long which has significant theoretical contributions to the governance theory with an Asian perspective and practical implications for administration and policy reform and innovation.

Local Government Innovativeness in China
Youlang Zhang

Talent Strategies and Leadership Development of the Public Sector
Insights from Southeast Asia
Celia Lee

Sustainable Development Goal 3
Health and Well-being of Ageing in Hong Kong
Ben Y. F. Fong and Vincent T. S. Law

Mainland China's Taiwan Policy
From Peaceful Development to Selective Engagement
Xin Qiang

For more information about this series, please visit www.routledge.com/Routledge-Focus-on-Public-Governance-in-Asia/book-series/RFPGA

Mainland China's Taiwan Policy

From Peaceful Development to Selective Engagement

Xin Qiang

Routledge
Taylor & Francis Group

LONDON AND NEW YORK

First published 2022
by Routledge
4 Park Square, Milton Park, Abingdon, Oxon OX14 4RN

and by Routledge
605 Third Avenue, New York, NY 10158

Routledge is an imprint of the Taylor & Francis Group, an informa business

British Library Cataloguing-in-Publication Data
A catalogue record for this book is available from the British Library

Library of Congress Cataloging-in-Publication Data
A catalog record has been requested for this book

ISBN: 978-0-367-75630-7 (hbk)
ISBN: 978-0-367-75629-1 (pbk)
ISBN: 978-1-003-16327-5 (ebk)

DOI: 10.4324/9781003163275

Typeset in Times New Roman
by Deanta Global Publishing Services, Chennai, India

Contents

Figures

Tables

1 Introduction
The turbulent Taiwan Strait

Few issues are as crucial to international security and East Asia's regional stability as the Taiwan issue – particularly in light of the inherent geostrategic risks and great power competition associated with the island that could potentially lead to a devastating conflict between two nuclear-armed states. Ever since the Democratic Progress Party (DPP), a pro-independence party on Taiwan Island, won the 2016 and 2020 presidential elections, relations between mainland China and Taiwan have been under intense strain, constantly exacerbated by repeated confrontations amidst a strained US–China relationship.

On October 1, 2021, when China started celebrating the seven-day holiday commemorating the National Day of the People's Republic of China (PRC), a six-state naval formation composing 17 warships, including 2 US aircraft carriers – the USS *Ronald Reagan* and USS *Carl Vinson* – was deployed to the waters adjacent to the Taiwan Island to conduct a military exercise. The military fleet was accompanied by the Royal Navy's aircraft carrier HMS *Queen Elizabeth* of the United Kingdom and helicopter carrier JS *Ise* of the Maritime Self-Defense Force of Japan. When the exercise kicked off on October 1, Kathleen Hicks, US deputy secretary of defense of the Biden administration, remarked at a virtual event at the Center for Strategic and International Studies (CSIS) that the US was monitoring the situation in Taiwan "very carefully" and that it had "a significant amount of capability forward in the region to tamp down" China's ambitions.[1]

Unsurprisingly, the exercise, which was held amid growing tensions between Beijing and Washington as well as between Beijing and Taipei, drew a furious reaction from Beijing. In response to the high-profile muscle-flexing of the US-led armada of allied ships, the Chinese People's Liberation Army (PLA) Air Force flew an unprecedented 150 sorties and entered the southwestern air defense identification zone (ADIZ) claimed by Taipei over a four-day period beginning on October 1.[2] It was reported by Taipei's Ministry of Defense that on October 1, the PLA deployed 38 warplanes,

DOI: 10.4324/9781003163275-1

followed by another 39 on October 2.[3] On October 3, US State Department spokesman Ned Price issued a statement claiming that Beijing's military activity "is destabilizing, risks miscalculations, and undermines regional peace and stability," pledging that the "American commitment to Taiwan is rock solid."[4] Subsequently, Taiwanese Foreign Minister Joseph Wu told Australian broadcaster ABC on October 4 in an interview that "if China is going to launch a war against Taiwan, we will fight to the end, and that is our commitment."[5] Despite the alert raised by Taiwanese officials about the readiness of Taiwan for war, 56 aircrafts, including H-6 bombers, KJ-500 airborne early warning airplanes, Y-8 anti-submarine warfare crafts, and J-16D and SU-30 fighter jets, were sent by the PLA toward Taiwan on October 4 alone, setting a new record for the scale of PLA's aerial operations over the Taiwan Strait. The Taiwan Air Force responded to this by issuing radio warnings, mobilizing air defense assets, and scrambling planes to monitor the mainland Chinese aircraft.

In the evening of October 5, Carlos Del Toro, the US chief of naval operations, proclaimed that the goal of the US is to prevent the mainland from attacking Taiwan, and that "if China is going to launch an attack against Taiwan, they are going to suffer tremendously as well," as he was introducing a strategic guidance at the US Naval Academy (USNA).[6] On October 6, an article written by Tsai Ing-wen, leader of the Taiwan administration, was published by the bimonthly journal *Foreign Affairs* with the title of "President of Taiwan," presenting a new overt challenge to the one-China principle insisted for decades by Beijing as the key political foundation for cross-Taiwan Strait relations.[7] The publication of Tsai's article came out alongside criticisms from US Secretary of State Antony Blinken on October 6, who reiterated concerns that Beijing was undermining regional peace and stability with "provocative action" and urged Beijing "to cease its military, diplomatic and economic pressure and coercion directed at Taiwan."[8] On the same day, in the face of Beijing's military pressure campaign, Chiu Kuo-cheng, Taiwan's defense minister, raised the alarm that military tensions between Taipei and Beijing were at a 40-year high and that the risk of an accidental "misfire" was growing.[9] In the evening, a proposal of an extra budget of US$8.7 billion over the next five years to upgrade and boost Taiwan's asymmetric warfare capabilities, including developing indigenous warships, and long-range and mobile missiles, was passed by the Foreign Affairs and National Defense Committee of Taiwan's Legislative Yuan.

Just one day later (October 7), Jake Sullivan, US national security adviser, told the BBC in Brussels that the US will "stand up for its friends" and that "we are going to take action now to try to prevent that day from ever coming to pass," when he was asked whether the US was prepared to take military behaviors to "defend Taiwan."[10] William Burns, the director of the Central

Intelligence Agency (CIA), announced the establishment of a new China Mission Center, whose purview includes assessing Beijing's intentions and activities over Taiwan, to "further strengthen our collective work on the most important geopolitical threat we face in the 21st Century – an increasingly adversarial Chinese government.".[11] A news report published by the *Wall Street Journal* on October 7 added fuel to the tension, quoting from a Pentagon official that a small unit of US special operations forces and a contingent of Marines have been secretly stationed in Taiwan for at least a year with the aim of instructing Taiwan ground forces on how to bolster the island defense and repel a possible attack by the mainland. It was the first time the US had publicly released or verified news about the deployment of US forces in Taiwan.[12] The presence of US military forces was unsurprisingly deemed by Beijing as a violation of China–US agreements on the one-China principle based on the three Sino-US Joint Communiques.[13] Responding to this, the Foreign Ministry of the PRC immediately expressed outrage at a daily news briefing, warning that China "would take all necessary measures to safeguard its sovereignty and territorial integrity" and urging the US to abide by the one-China principle, which is "the political foundation of Sino-US relations."[14] On October 7, the chairman of the American Institute in Taiwan (AIT), James Moriarty, vowed to help Taipei to maintain sufficient self-defense capacities and develop asymmetric warfare capabilities against the "real and imminent" threat from Beijing.[15]

On October 8, Taiwan's foreign minister, Joseph Wu, claimed that Taiwan should not be "falsely" excluded from the United Nations (UN) and "it is a common expectation for Taiwan to participate in the UN" since the United Nations General Assembly 2758 (XXVI) passed in 1971 had not denied Taiwan's representation in the UN.[16] Outraged by the aforementioned moves of Tsai's administration and the US, China's president, Xi Jinping, fired back on October 9 at a commemorative meeting marking the 110th anniversary of the Revolution of 1911, stating that Taiwan's independence "was a grave lurking threat to national rejuvenation." President Xi further stated that "external forces should respect China's sovereignty, security and development interests," and that "no one should underestimate the Chinese people's strong will, determination, and ability to defend national sovereignty and territorial integrity."[17] On the same day, Taiwan's army commander, Hsu Yen-pu, flew to the US for a series of secret meetings with top officials of the Pentagon and General Alberto Aquilino, commander of the Indo-Pacific Command, to further enhance US–Taiwan military cooperation.

On October 10, one day after Xi's speech, Tsai delivered an address at "Taiwan National Day 2021" celebrations and repeatedly emphasized the "72-year history" of the "Republic of China Taiwan." She also asserted, for the first time, that Taiwan will insist on the "enduring commitment" that "the Republic of China and the People's Republic of China should not be subordinate to each other (*hubu lishu*)."[18] Tsai's statement was blasted by the Taiwan Affairs Office (TAO) of the PRC that the cross-Strait relations are by no means "state to state relations," therefore the claims made by Tsai were "an unclad peddle of the 'Two States Thesis.'"[19] Tsai's address was followed by a large-scale military parade displaying several types of missiles, including the Thunderbolt 2000 multiple rocket launcher, and the medium-range Sky Sword II and Sky Bow III, as well as cruise missiles Hsiung Feng II and III. On the same day of Tsai's speech, the army and navy battle groups under the leadership of the Eastern Theater Command of the PLA started amphibious landing combat exercises and live-fire maneuvers along the southern coast of Fujian Province, the closest mainland province, which lies 100 miles off the Taiwan coast, sending a "solemn warning" to the Taiwanese "secessionist factions" and their "foreign backers."

In the space of just ten days in early October 2021, cross-Strait relations witnessed another round of finger-pointing rhetoric and military posturing. Even worse, these threatening moves were simply a sketchy footage of a long chain of escalating tit-for-tat between Beijing and Taipei, and doubtlessly came at a particularly tense and competitive time for relations between China and the US. Amid the heightened tensions, many Western officials, generals, and observers believed Beijing is changing, or even has already changed, its long-term "peaceful unification policy" and is ready, or even willing, to use force to achieve national reunification shortly. For example, Admiral Philip Davidson, then commander of the US Indo-Pacific Command, gave his prescient warning to the Senate Foreign Relations Committee in March 2021 that the mainland was likely to attack Taiwan "in the next six years."[20] The current cross-Strait situation was also described "as the most serious" by Minister Chiu Kuo-cheng, adding that Beijing already had the ability to attack the island and would be completely prepared to mount a "full-scale" attack with minimal losses by 2025 with regard to the ability of the PLA.[21]

It is obviously not groundless for the *Economist* to label Taiwan as "the most dangerous place on earth."[22] Nonetheless, military warnings aside, it is also noteworthy that President Xi reiterated in his October 9 address that "peaceful reunification of the motherland best serves the overall interests of the Chinese nation, including the Taiwan compatriots," and reaffirmed that "we have adhered to the basic principle of peaceful reunification of one country, two systems, the one-China principle and the '1992 Consensus', and have promoted the peaceful development of cross-Strait relations."[23] It echoed Xi's pledge to "promote the peaceful reunification of the motherland" with Taiwan compatriots in his speech given at the ceremony celebrating the 100th anniversary of the founding of the Communist Party of China (CPC) on July 1, 2021.[24] In a virtual meeting with US President Joe Biden on November 16, Xi emphasized again that "we will strive for the prospect of peaceful reunification with utmost sincerity and efforts." [25]

In spite of the extending political impasse and military tension, cross-Strait economic and trade exchanges boomed even if shadowed by the outbreak of the COVID-19 pandemic. According to the statistics released by China's General Administration of Customs on October 13, 2021, trade volume between the mainland and Taiwan from January to September in 2021 was US\$239.52 billion, of which the mainland imported US\$182.47 billion from Taiwan, up 28.9% from the previous year. Notably, in the first three quarters of 2021, Taiwan's trade surplus with the mainland topped US\$120 billion.[26] With these figures in mind, can we then still be certain that cross-Strait relations are hurtling to the edge of a potential crisis or are indeed on the verge of a preordained military conflict? How and to what extent would such a robust economic relationship impact on the likelihood of military conflict between mainland China and Taiwan?

It is no exaggeration to say that mainland China's relation to Taiwan has been in constant contention since the founding of the PRC in October 1949, when Chiang Kai-shek's Kuomintang (KMT), or the Chinese Nationalist Party, was ousted from mainland China. As a legacy of the CPC–KMT civil war, the 1950s witnessed the outburst of two bloody Taiwan Strait Crises. Fortunately, given the fact that both sides were defenders of the one-China principle, the cross-Strait relationship did not deteriorate into sanguinary conflict in the 1960s and 1970s in spite of the enduring historic hostility.

Starting in the 1980s, when Beijing decided to pursue economic reform and the policy of opening up, the mainland turned to cultivate closer economic and social ties with Taiwan in the hope of peacefully unifying with the island under the "one country, two systems" framework. The resumption of dialogues on a semiofficial basis between the two sides shed a ray of light on the frosty cross-Strait relations. However, the outbreak of the Third Taiwan Strait Crisis following the visit of Lee Teng-hui's visit to the US in 1995, and Chen Shuibian's successive election victories in 2000 and 2004, drove cross-Strait relations to rock bottom and spiked continuous tension. In the face of Lee's shift away from KMT's commitment to the one-China principle and Chen's pro-independence policy, Beijing had to return to a blanket "little-contact" or even "no-contact" policy to address the cross-Strait standoff.

After May 2008, when the island was ruled by Ma Ying-jeou of the KMT, the pro-one China party, Beijing began to adopt a much more constructive and accommodating approach to Ma's administration, in sharp contrast with its tougher approach in dealing with the Chen Shuibian administration from 2000 to 2008. Correspondingly, Beijing formulated a policy framework of "peaceful development" to enhance comprehensive cooperation between the two sides. With mutual effort from both Beijing and Taipei, cross-Strait relations thereafter sailed into a remarkable peaceful development period.

However, the momentum was reversed after the DPP's Tsai Ing-wen won the presidency in 2016 and was reelected in 2020. Since the inauguration of Tsai on May 20, 2016, Beijing, under the leadership of Xi Jinping, has dramatically changed its accommodative tune and turned to pursue a "selective engagement" policy aiming to pressure Taipei to accept the one-China principle. Unsurprisingly, Beijing's pressure campaign was met forcefully by Taipei, as well as Washington, which moved to define Beijing as a vital strategic adversary. The tit-for-tat between the two sides triggered ever-increasing tensions across the Strait, amid the troubling escalation of the broader US–China rivalry.

As the cross-Strait relationship deteriorates and derails from a track of comprehensive cooperation and negotiated rapprochement to a new cycle of grim political standoffs and dangerous military friction, the whole region is watching with bated breath, worrying whether the fragile status quo, namely "no unification, no independence, no war," can be maintained across the Taiwan Strait. Therefore, it is more crucial than ever to examine and answer the following important questions based on a rational understanding and accurate interpretation of Beijing's Taiwan policymaking mentality and thinking. What is the consistent mainstream policymaking mentality of Beijing's policy transition? What are the principal features of Beijing's Taiwan policy to cope with the KMT and the DPP administrations? What are the driving dynamics for Beijing's Taiwan policy adjustments in different periods featuring fundamental shifts from confrontation to cooperation, then back to confrontation again? What are the underlying strategic continuities beneath the apparent policy changes of Beijing? How will Beijing's Taiwan policy evolve and develop with its ever-growing national power? How and to what extent will the intensifying US–China strategic rivalry influence Beijing's Taiwan policy and the prospect of cross-Strait relations in the near future?

With these questions in mind, the present book aims at providing some clues to unlock the aforementioned puzzles from the perspective of a mainland Chinese observer. Chapter 2 examines Beijing's peaceful development policy to Taipei after Ma Ying-jeou came into office in 2008. It points out that with the reestablishment of political mutual trust based on the 1992 Consensus, Beijing and Taipei expeditiously resumed quasi-official and semiofficial dialogue and communication culminated by the Xi–Ma Summit in Singapore; reached a long list of agreements ranging from economic, financial, cultural, educational, and social to judiciary cooperation; and fulfilled an all-dimensional détente even in sensitive military and diplomatic areas. By tracing the evolution of the peaceful development policy initiated by President Hu Jintao and succeeded by President Xi Jiping, this chapter discusses the reasons for the introduction of the policy, as well as the result and influence of the policy in cross-Strait political, diplomatic, economic, financial, social, and security relations.

Chapter 3 explores Beijing's "selective engagement" policy framework after Tsai Ying-wen overwhelmingly won the presidency in May 2016 and consistently repudiated the one-China principle. On one hand, Beijing increased pressure upon the Tsai administration on security, political, and diplomatic frontiers to deter Taipei from pursuing an independence-leaning agenda, in addition to the precision-targeting of various "separatist forces" to contain the Taiwan independence momentum on the island. On the other hand, Beijing continued to encourage cross-Strait economic, social, and cultural exchanges to maintain the civil cooperation dynamics between the two sides, in addition to strengthening engagement with a wide spectrum of non-pro-independence forces to check and balance possible Taiwan independence ventures. Behaviors, leverages, effects, and challenges concerning this dual-track policy framework will be observed and discussed in this chapter.

Chapter 4 aims to elucidate the inherent policymaking mindset of mainland China, expounding the strategic and tactical changes and continuities behind the transitions of Beijing's Taiwan policy. By answering three vital questions, this chapter argues that given the political reality on the island, Beijing had changed its prominent concern from "pursuant of de jure Taiwan independence" to "perpetuation of de facto Taiwan independence," as well as changed its guideline for fulfilling reunification from "placing hope on the Taiwanese" to "placing more hope on the mainland itself." Meanwhile, Beijing continues to focus on the accomplishment of comprehensive modernization within its overarching timetable for "national rejuvenation," which means the resolution of the Taiwan issue is not yet the top priority on the mainland's two-centennial strategic agenda, and Beijing still prefers to achieve peaceful reunification unless Taipei would pursue a radical de jure independence policy.

The final chapter (Chapter 5) summarizes the key conclusions drawn from the prior chapters and ventures to discuss the future of Beijing's Taiwan policy as well as its potential implication on the cross-Taiwan Strait situation, the regional security landscape, and China–US relationship. The chapter concludes with policy suggestions aimed at resuming the positive-sum dynamics among the three stakeholders, i.e., Beijing, Taipei, and Washington.

Notes

1 "A Conversation with Deputy Secretary of Defense Dr. Kathleen H. Hicks," CSIS, October 1, 2021, https://www.csis.org/analysis/conversation-deputy-secretary-defense-dr-kathleen-h-hicks.

2 ADIZ is normally a designated area of airspace declared by a nation-state to allow it to identify, locate, and control approaching foreign aircraft for security concerns, but such zones are not considered territorial airspace. Geographically, Taiwan's self-declared ADIZ overlaps with mainland China, both its territorial waters and actual land. What's more, mainland China had never accepted the ADIZ of Taiwan because Taiwan is not a state that has the legal right to claim "sovereignty space" or ADIZ according to the one-China principle.

3 The previous deployment record was 28 Chinese aircraft flying into the ADIZ of Taiwan set in June 2021.

4 Ned Price, "Department Press Briefing – October 4, 2021," US Department of State, October 4, 2021, https://www.state.gov/briefings/department-press-briefing-october-04-2021-2.

5 Andrew Greene and Stan Grant, "Taiwanese Foreign Minister Warns His Country Is Preparing for War with China, Asks Australia for Help," ABC, October 3, 2021, https://www.abc.net.au/news/2021-10-04/taiwan-preparing -for-war-with-china/100511294.

6 Megan Eckstein, "Navy Secretary's New Strategic Guidance Focuses on Deterring China from Invading Taiwan," *Defense News*, October 6, 2021, https://www.defensenews.com/naval/2021/10/05/navy-secretarys-new-strategic-guidance-focuses-on-deterring-china-from-invading-taiwan.

7 Tsai Ing-wen, "Taiwan and the Fight for Democracy," *Foreign Affairs* 100, no. 6 (November–December 2021), 74–84.

8 "Secretary Antony J. Blinken and OECD Secretary-General Mathias Cormann at a Joint Press Availability," US Department of State, October 6, 2021, https:// www.state.gov/secretary-antony-j-blinken-and-oecd-secretary-general-mathias -cormann-at-a-joint-press-availability.

9 Nicolas Smith, "China Could Invade Taiwan in Three Years, Warns Defence Chief," *Telegraph*, October 6, 2021, https://www.telegraph.co.uk/world-news /2021/10/06/joe-biden-says-china-agrees-abide-taiwan-agreement.

10 James Landale, "US Deeply Concerned over Taiwan-China Tension," BBC, October 7, 2021, https://www.bbc.com/news/world-us-canada-58837432.

11 Julian Barnes, "CIA Reorganization to Place New Focus on China," *New York Times*, October 8, 2021, https://cn.nytimes.com/usa/20211008/cia-reorganization-china/dual.

12 See Gordon Lubold, "US Troops Have Been Deployed in Taiwan for at Least a Year," *Wall Street Journal*, October 7, 2021, https://www.wsj.com/articles/u-s -troops-have-been-deployed-in-taiwan-for-at-least-a-year-11633614043. Defense authorities from the US and Taiwan administrations declined to comment on the matter. However, neither side denied the report, with Pentagon spokesman John Supple reiterating US support for Taiwan against mainland China.

13 When the two countries officially established diplomatic relations in 1979, the US agreed that it would sever its "diplomatic relations" with Taiwan, withdraw US military forces from Taiwan, and terminate the Mutual Defense Treaty. The aforementioned three points were the premise for Beijing and Washington to establish diplomatic ties. In the Joint Communiqué on the Establishment of

Diplomatic Relations between Washington and Beijing, the US pledged that it would only maintain cultural, commercial, and other unofficial relations with the people of Taiwan.

14 Zhao Jia, "Washington's Help for Taiwan Forces Criticized," *China Daily*, October 9, 2021, https://www.chinadaily.com.cn/a/202110/09/WS6160f7baa 310cdd39bc6dc64.html; "Foreign Ministry Spokesperson Zhao Lijian's Regular Press Conference on October 8, 2021," Ministry of Foreign Affairs of the People's Republic of China, October 8, 2021, https://www.fmprc.gov.cn/mfa_eng/xwfw _665399/s2510_665401/2511_665403/202110/t20211008_9580321.html.

15 Matthew Strong, "American Institute in Taiwan Chairman Calls Chinese Threat Real and Imminent," *Taiwan News*, October 7, 2021, https://www.taiwannews .com.tw/en/news/4308607.

16 Zhou Zhihao, "The Fight to Return to the United Nations, Joseph Wu: The United Nations General Assembly 2758 Did Not Mention Taiwan," *United Daily News*, October 8, 2021, https://udn.com/news/story/6656/5803368.

17 The Revolution of 1911, also known as the Xinhai Revolution, happened on October 10, 1991. Under the leadership of nationalist Dr. Sun Yat-sen, it over-threw the Qing dynasty, ended more than 2,000 years of imperial rule in China, and founded the Republic of China. In Taiwan, the date of the uprising, October 10, has been celebrated as the national day of the Republic of China ever since 1912. For Xi's speech, see "Xinhua Commentary: A New Warning to Taiwan Separatists and Their Supporters," Xinhua News Agency, October 9, 2021, http://www.news.cn/english/2021-10/09/c_1310235109.htm.

18 Central News Agency, "Taiwan President Tsai Ing-wen's National Day Speech (Full Text)," *Taiwan Times*, October 10, 2021, https://www.taiwannews.com.tw /en/news/4311090.

19 October 10 is the legal National Day of the Republic of China. Even though the Chinese title of the celebration was "110th National Day of the ROC," the English translation that appeared on the ceremony on this day was "Taiwan National Day 2021." For the official remarks from PRC, see "Taiwan Affairs Office Commented on the So-Called 'Speech' of the Democratic Progressive Party Leader: Advocating 'Taiwan Independence' and Inciting Confrontation," Taiwan Affairs Office of the State Council, October 10, 2021, http://www.gwytb .gov.cn/xwdt/xwfb/wyly/202110/t20211010_12383506.htm. Also see "Press Conference Series on October 13, 2021," Taiwan Affairs Office of the State Council, October 13, 2021, http://www.gwytb.gov.cn/xwdt/xwfb/xwfbh/202110 /t20211013_12384220.htm.

20 Brad Lendon, "China Building Offensive, Aggressive Military, Top US Pacific Commander Says," CNN, March 10, 2021, https://www.cnn.com/2021/03/10/ asia/us-pacific-commander-china-threat-intl-hnk-ml/index.html; Oriana Mastro, "The Taiwan Temptation: Why Beijing Might Resort to Force," *Foreign Affairs* 100, no. 4 (July–August 2021), 58–67.

21 Lo Tien-pin and Aaron Tu, "Military Tensions Worst in 40 years: Chiu," *Taipei Times*, October 7, 2021, https://www.taipeitimes.com/News/front/archives/2021 /10/07/2003765671.

22 "The Most Dangerous Place on Earth," *Economist*, May 1, 2021, https://www .economist.com/leaders/2021/05/01/the-most-dangerous-place-on-earth.

23 "Xi Jinping: Remarks on the 110th Anniversary of the Revolution of 1911," Xinhua News Agency, October 9, 2021, http://www.news.cn/politics/leaders /2021-10/09/c_1127941568.htm.

24 "Xi Jinping: Remarks on the Centenary of the CPC," July 1, 2021, http://www.xinhuanet.com/politics/leaders/2021-07/15/c_1127658385.htm.
25 "President Xi Jinping Had a Virtual Meeting with US President Joe Biden," Ministry of Foreign Affairs of PRC, November 16, 2021, https://www.fmprc.gov.cn/mfa_eng/zxxx_662805/202111/t20211116_10448843.html.
26 "Imports and Exports of Goods in the Main Countries (Regions): The Total Value Table (in US Dollars)," General Administration of Customs of PRC, October 13, 2021, http://www.customs.gov.cn/customs/302249/zfxxgk/2799825/302274/302275/3946693/index.html.

2 Peaceful development

Mainland China's institutionalism-oriented Taiwan policy (2008–2016)

Introduction

The stalemate across the Taiwan Strait following the 2000 Taiwan presidential election and the pro-independence policies of Chen Shuibian's Democratic Progress Party (DPP) administration have thrown cross-Strait relations into a dangerous downward spiral. Nonetheless, starting from the "Five-Point Vision" issued in the Hu Jintao–Lien Chan April 2005 joint statement, to the new concept of "Common Destiny Community" (*mingyun gongtongti*) advocated in the report to 17th National Congress of the Communist Party of China (CPC) in October 2007, and to the "16-character guideline" proposed by President Hu in April 2008, some evident clues could be detected that Beijing had attempted to outline a more accommodating and flexible Taiwan policy framework featuring peaceful development.[1]

The Kuomintang (KMT) victory in the 2008 presidential election on the island and Ma Ying-jeou's adherence to one-China principle, though Taipei always emphasized the "respective interpretation" of "one China," had created essential conditions for the warming of cross-Strait relations. After many years of tensions resulting from the changing political and social situation on Taiwan Island, mainland China had conducted a wave of policy adjustments that provided powerful dynamics for the improvement of cross-Strait relations. As a result, authorities and civilians on the Chinese mainland and Taiwan had witnessed unprecedented détente and remarkable progress in cross-Straits relations through the shelving of divergences, engagement in extensive exchanges and the increase of cooperation.

Initiation of Beijing's peaceful development policy

The declarations of Ye Jianying's "Nine-Point Proposal" (*ye jiutiao*) in 1981 and Deng Xiaoping's "one country, two systems" formula in 1982 marked the greatest transition of Beijing's Taiwan strategy in a new

DOI: 10.4324/9781003163275-2

era when economic modernization had been made the foremost goal of mainland China. From then on, "peaceful reunification" become the official narrative of the mainland, which continued on to the "Eight Points of Jiang Zemin" (*jiang badian*) in 1995 and then to the "Four Opinions of Hu Jintao" (*hu sidian*) in 2005. All of these reflected the successive development and evolution of Beijing's strategic thinking upon the Taiwan issue. In carrying out this policy, mainland China had gradually discarded and moved beyond its conventional antagonistic mentality, and increasingly strode toward the promotion of a system of cross-Strait cooperation and mutual benefit, so as to eventually undertake a peaceful reunification.

For instance, on January 1, 1979, the Standing Committee of the National People's Congress (NPC), the mainland's top legislature, published a proposal calling for the opening of direct transport, trade, and mail services across the Taiwan Strait, that is, the so-called Three Links (*santong*). That same year, the mainland began providing mail, telegraph, and telephone services to Taiwan. Encouraged by a range of preferential policies issued by the mainland, economic cooperation and social exchanges across the Strait began to grow rapidly, especially after the lifting of Taiwan's curfew in 1987. In 1991, Beijing established the Association for Relations Across the Taiwan Straits (ARATS), a quasi-official institution, to negotiate with its counterpart, Taipei's Straits Exchange Foundation (SEF), to handle cross-Strait affairs. In November 1992, ARATS and SEF held talks in Hong Kong and reached what has been subsequently tagged as the "1992 Consensus," thus paving the way for the historic Wang–Koo meeting in Singapore in April 1993 and the signing of four agreements on cross-Strait cooperation.

In 1996, telecommunications service providers from the two sides jointly established direct services. In 1997, the mainland cities of Fuzhou and Xiamen, and the city of Kaohsiung in Taiwan operated direct sailing trials across the Strait. In 2001, passenger and cargo shipments opened between Taiwan's Kimmen and Matsu islands, and the mainland's Fujian Province. In January 2003, the first one-way "Spring Festival direct charter flights" flew from Taipei, transiting in Hong Kong, and landed in Shanghai. In the handling of these measures and policies, Beijing had tried to extend amity and goodwill to Taipei by facilitating trade links and personnel exchanges between both sides, working hard to guide cross-Strait relations into a constructive channel.

Although demoralized by the pro-independence policies advocated by the Lee Teng-hui and Chen Shuibian administrations, which resulted in a longstanding stalemate of cross-Strait political interactions and, occasionally, intensified military tension, Beijing had not abandoned its aim of peaceful reunification through cross-Strait institutional cooperation and mutually beneficial development. For example, on March 4, 2005, President Hu outlined the possibility of establishing a "framework for peaceful and stable cross-Strait development" through mutual consultation and negotiation.[2] In accordance with this appeal, Beijing extended an olive branch to pan-Blue Camp[3] in order to break the cross-Strait stalemate in flank. As the pioneer of CPC–KMT high-level exchanges, then KMT vice chairman Chiang Pin-kung visited Guangzhou City in March 2005, the first official visit to the mainland by a vice chairman-level leader of the KMT in 60 years. In Beijing, then Chinese People's Political Consultative Conference (CPPCC) chairman Jia Qinglin conveyed to Chiang an invitation from President Hu for Lien Chan, the then chairman of the KMT.

On April 26, 2005, a delegation led by then KMT chairman Lien Chan landed in Nanjing, launching the first such visit to mainland China in 60 years. Lien's groundbreaking visit culminated in his April 29 meeting with General Secretary Hu in Beijing, the first meeting since 1945 between the top leaders of the CPC and the KMT. On this historical occasion, the two parties issued five points of compromise on the premise of acknowledging the 1992 Consensus.[4] In the subsequent joint communiqué titled "Shared Vision for the Cross-Strait Peaceful Development," Beijing put forward the idea of "peaceful development" for the first time and expressed its hopes that a series of institutional arrangements could be reached constructively, including the formal conclusion to the decades of cross-Strait antagonism; immediate and comprehensive cross-Strait economic cooperation; complete, immediate, bilateral realization of the Three Links; establishment of a stable and secure system for cooperation; and discussion of a cross-Strait common market.[5]

Following Lien's visit, James Soong, chairman of the People First Party and prominent figure of the pan-blue camp, started his own nine-day visit to the mainland in May. The two parties reached a consensus on six issues after the Hu–Soong meeting on defining the establishment of mechanisms for cross-Strait military trust and economic cooperation, hastening cross-Strait trade normalization, negotiating long-term cooperation institutions, and discussing Taiwan's participation in international organizations.[6]

The aforementioned friendly interactions injected new vitality into stagnant cross-Strait ties and encouraged Beijing to continue its policy adjustments. On April 16, 2006, President Hu advocated for the first time that "peaceful development should be the theme of cross-Strait relations and the common goal for both sides."[7] From then on, "peaceful development" has become the most frequently quoted phrase and the guideline for Beijing's cross-Strait policies. In the report to the 17th CPC National Congress, Hu called upon the two sides to "build a framework for the peaceful development of cross-Strait relations" and "create a new situation for the peaceful development of cross-Strait relations."[8] One month before Ma's inauguration, Beijing proposed again in April 2008 to build mutual trust, create a win–win situation, and called for further development of economic cooperative institutions.

Despite the obstruction and opposition from Chen's administration then in power, Beijing had also tried its best to promote cross-Strait exchanges and cooperation in line with these new policy ideas. For example, driven by mainland China, the first non-stop two-way direct charter flight across the Strait was launched on January 29, 2005, during the Spring Festival holiday, and for the first time in 56 years airlines from mainland China were allowed to land on Taiwan. In June 2006, the two sides reached a consensus on the framework of charter flights, which agreed to open charter flights for more traditional festivals in addition to the Spring Festival and for other special cases.[9] Under domestic pressure, Chen's administration reluctantly expressed its openness to a possible "tour group model" for mainland tourists visiting Taiwan in February 2007.[10] In conjunction with Taipei's policy signal, Beijing immediately drafted the "Blueprint for Mainland Residents Traveling to the Taiwan Area," so as to detail the relevant regulations and accommodate the necessary requirements.[11]

On July 18, 2005, Beijing gave formal approval to the construction of a comprehensive system of Cross-Strait (Fujian) Agricultural Cooperation Experimental Zones to explore cross-Strait cooperation on agriculture, fishery, and water resources. Shortly afterward, Beijing unilaterally announced the removal of customs duties on 15 major kinds of fruits imported from Taiwan, including pineapple, coconut, and mango, dating from August 1, 2005. Since May 31, 2006, a "green channel" road network in the mainland has been made available to facilitate the transportation of agricultural products from Taiwan.[12] From then on, Beijing consecutively put forward more than 80 one-way preferential policies toward Taipei, such as the expansion of agricultural investment, promotion of Taiwanese agricultural produce in the mainland market, simplification of immigration procedures, equal fees and standards for Taiwanese students studying in the mainland and scholarships for Taiwanese students, the promotion of opportunities for Taiwanese seeking employment, and financing for Taiwanese enterprises seeking development in the mainland.

The Ma administration's adherence to the 1992 Consensus created the necessary conditions for turning these cooperative initiatives on paper into practical policy. Coordinating with the improved cross-Strait situation and positive gestures displayed by the Ma administration, President Hu offered "Six Proposals" to encourage both sides to increase communication and exchanges in all circles including economic, political, diplomatic, and security issues, and promised that the mainland would actively respond to any constructive proposals from Taiwan that would boost peaceful development across the Strait.[13] Along with the continuous development in trade and economic connections and the increasing interflow of personnel between both sides, Beijing gradually went beyond the traditional confrontational thinking adopted to deal with the Lee and Chen administrations toward advancing cross-Strait mutual development through nurturing stabilized confidence and developing institutionalized cooperative mechanisms. Beijing's peaceful development policy, welcomed and collaborated by Taipei, ushered cross-Strait relations into a new era featuring comprehensive détente and booming cooperation.

Xiaobu kuaipao: Implementation of Beijing's peaceful development policy

The relentless advocacy of peaceful development by Beijing suggested a new mindset on the Taiwan issue. Frustrated by Lee's and Chen's independence-leaning policies, Beijing tried to take the opportunity provided byMa's presidency to comprehensively improve cross-Strait ties and promote final reunification. Under the overarching concept of peaceful development, Beijing conducted a variety of policy adjustments, cautiously but not necessarily slowly, in a pattern of *xiaobu kuaipao*, that is, running fast but with small steps. Through efforts from the two sides, cross-Strait negotiations had been resumed, institutionalized arrangements established, various agreements reached, and full-blown détente fulfilled. The constructive interaction between Beijing and Taipei led to a series of crucial progress and a new positive landscape for cross-Strait relationship.

First, cross-Strait economic and trade cooperation were greatly enhanced. Inspired by vigorous cross-Strait economic and trade development in spite of political friction, Beijing believed the institutionalization of economic cooperation would provide a stronger impetus for the peaceful development of cross-Strait relations.[14] Following the modus operandi of "separation of politics and economy" (*zhengjing fenli*) and "economy and trade first" (*jingmao youxian*), Beijing reached a slew of agreements with Taipei to establish an economic cooperation mechanism and promote cross-Strait economic and trade exchanges. The Economic Cooperation Framework Agreement (ECFA), signed on June 29, 2010, was widely regarded as the most significant agreement. The agreement, much more preferential to Taipei, reduced tariffs and commercial barriers between the two sides by cutting tariffs on 539 Taiwanese exports to the mainland and 267 mainland products entering Taiwan. It was estimated that almost US$14 billion of Taiwanese goods exported to the mainland had their tariffs reduced or removed, while mainland exports worth just under US$3 billion enjoyed lower or zero tariffs in order to appease Taiwan's economic concerns.[15]

As the first-ever comprehensive economic agreement between the two sides, the ECFA laid down the cornerstone for the normalization of cross-Strait economic cooperation by establishing an institutional framework.[16]

Encouraged and supported by the cross-Strait institutional arrangement, cross-Strait trade rushed in the fast lane and grew from US$129.2 billion in 2008 to US$179.6 billion in 2016, while peaking in 2014 with the figure of US$198.3 billion (Figure 2.1 and Table 2.1).

On June 21, 2013, the Cross-Strait Service Trade Agreement (CSSTA), a major follow-up accord to the ECFA, was concluded. It aimed at normalizing and liberalizing cross-Strait trade in services, and in this agreement Beijing again made more concessions to Taipei. Under the terms of the agreement, service industries such as banking, healthcare, tourism, film, telecommunications, and publishing would be opened to cross-Strait investment. It reflected Beijing's intention to reinforce bilateral economic and trade links and embrace an era of full-scale "economic integration" across the Strait, an idea proposed by Premier Li Keqiang for the first time in his March 2014 government work report to the NPC.[17] One month later,

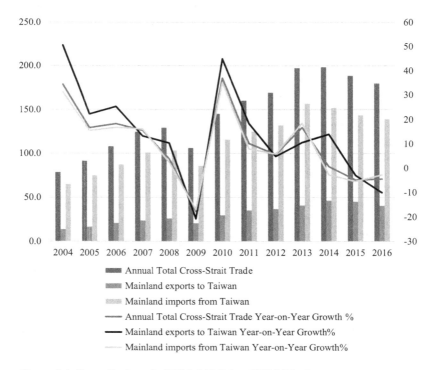

Figure 2.1 Cross-Strait trade (2004–2016) (per US$ billion).

Table 2.1 Cross-Strait trade (2004–2016) (per US$ billion)

Year	Annual total cross-Strait trade	Year-on-year growth (%)	Mainland exports to Taiwan	Year-on-year growth%	Mainland imports from Taiwan	Year-on-year growth (%)
2004	78.3	34.2	13.6	50.4	64.8	31.2
2005	91.2	16.5	16.6	22.2	74.7	15.3
2006	107.8	18.2	20.7	25.3	87.1	16.6
2007	124.5	15.4	23.5	13.1	101.0	16
2008	129.2	3.8	25.9	10.3	103.3	2.3
2009	106.2	−17.8	20.5	−20.8	85.7	−17
2010	145.4	36.9	29.7	44.8	115.7	35
2011	160.0	10.1	35.1	18.3	124.9	7.9
2012	169.0	5.6	36.8	4.8	132.2	5.8
2013	197.3	16.7	40.6	10.5	156.6	18.5
2014	198.3	0.6	46.3	13.9	152.0	−2.8
2015	188.6	−4.9	44.9	−3	143.7	−5.5
2016	179.6	−4.5	40.4	−10.1	139.2	−2.8

Source: The General Administration of Customs of PRC, Cross-Strait Trade Statistics by Year, http://www.gwytb.gov.cn/local/201805 /20180524_11958201.htm, access via the Taiwan Affairs Office of the State Council of PRC.

Li appealed to Vincent Siew at the Bo'ao Forum again to further expand economic cooperation and enhance economic integration.[18] However, contrary to Beijing's expectation, the palpable fear and anxiety over the CSSTA ignited confrontational reactions from Taiwanese who wanted to wean Taiwan's economic dependence off the mainland. The Sunflower Student Movement, backed by the DPP, finally drove the ratification process to a dead end in April 2014 after the Legislative Yuan had been occupied by protesters. What is more, the negotiation of another planned agreement, the Cross-Strait Goods Trade Agreement, had consequently grounded to a halt.

On the other hand, financial cooperation between the two sides achieved unprecedented breakthroughs. In order to help Taiwanese enterprises squeezed by the global economic crunch triggered by the US subprime financial crisis, Beijing unveiled ten beneficiary measures exclusively for Taiwanese businesspeople operating in the mainland in December 2008 to gain greater access to loans and restructure their operations, which immediately received a burst of applause from the island.[19] The Cross-Strait Financial Cooperation Agreement inked in April 2009 was appraised as a milestone for the institutionalization of financial cooperation. This agreement and three succeeding memorandums of understanding signed in November established a framework of cross-Strait financial cooperation allowing for two-way collaboration in supervision and management in the banking, securities and futures, and insurance industries. In April 2009, mainland's telecom giant, China Mobile Ltd., was allowed to invest US$528 million and buy 12% of Taiwan's third-largest telecom operator Far EasTone, the first direct investment by a mainland state-owned company in the island in six decades.[20] The Financial Supervisory Commission (FSC) of Taipei shortly started to permit mainland investors to invest in Taiwan's money markets for the first time since 1949 and apply to purchase Taiwan shares that did not exceed one-tenth of the value of the firm's total shares. Three mainland Chinese banks – the Bank of China, the Bank of Communications, and China Construction Bank – were admitted to establish branches in Taipei. In addition, numerous Taiwanese banks, including the First Commercial Bank, Cathay United Bank, and Bank of Taiwan, received the FSC's approval to set up branches or subsidiaries in the mainland. In November 2008, Fubon Bank (Hong Kong), the locally listed unit of Taiwan's Fubon Financial Holding, gained the mainland's approval to buy 19.99% of Xiamen City Commercial Bank for RMB 250 million, marking the first investment by a Taiwan-based company in a mainland lender and the largest single equity investment in a mainland bank by a Taiwanese-owned bank.[21] In sum, the establishment of a collaboration mechanism propelled the long-term and deeply embedded economic relationships across the Strait at an expanded and accelerated rate (Figure 2.2 and Table 2.2).[22]

Second, Beijing began to adopt a strategy of "diplomatic truce." Competition between the mainland and Taiwan for diplomatic allies has lasted for more than half a century. In order to fight against Taiwan's "legitimate independence," Beijing used to spare no effort to take away Taipei's few remaining allies. However, the diplomatic tug-of-war not only caused unnecessary waste of political and economic resources for both sides, but what was even worse was that every time a country allied with Taipei changed its diplomatic allegiance to Beijing, it would arouse dissatisfaction or anger in Taipei and slow the momentum of positive public opinion toward the mainland in Taiwan. It thereby contributed to Beijing's oft-stated willingness to make some "proper and reasonable arrangements for Taiwan's participation in international organizations" as long as it does not create the impression that there are "two Chinas" or "one China and one Taiwan."[23] Ma's unambiguous adherence to the one-China principle provided the fundamental dynamic for Beijing's policy shift. In December 2008, Hu for the first time proposed to "negotiate foreign-related affairs" so as to avoid both

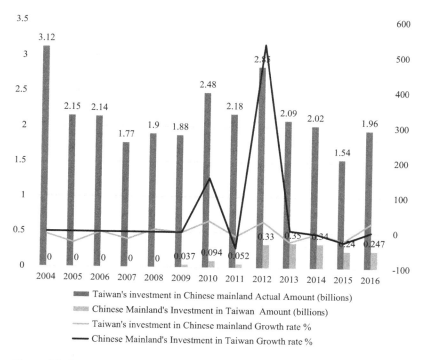

Figure 2.2 Cross-Strait investment (2004–2016) (per US$ billion).

Table 2.2 Cross-Strait investment (2004–2016) (per US$ billion)

Year	Taiwan's investment in Chinese mainland		Chinese mainland's investment in Taiwan	
	Actual amount (billions)	Growth rate (%)	Amount (billions)	Growth rate (%)
2004	3.12	−7.7	N/A	N/A
2005	2.15	−31	N/A	N/A
2006	2.14	−0.7	N/A	N/A
2007	1.77	−20.4	N/A	N/A
2008	1.9	7	N/A	N/A
2009	1.88	−1	0.037	N/A
2010	2.48	31.7	0.094	154.05
2011	2.18	−11.81	0.052	−44.68
2012	2.85	30.4	0.33	534.62
2013	2.09	−26.7	0.35	5.12
2014	2.02	−3.30	0.34	−4.01
2015	1.54	−23.80	0.24	−27.16
2016	1.96	27.7	0.247	1.64

Source: Ministry of the Commerce of PRC, Taiwan, Hong Kong and Macao Department, The Statistics of Mainland-Taiwan Trade and Economic Cooperation, 2020, http://tga.mof com.gov.cn/article/sjzl/taiwan.

Note: Investment transited from the third place is not included.

sides engaging in vicious competition and "unnecessary internal friction" in the international community.[24]

In response to Ma's call for a "diplomatic truce", a tacit understanding of suspending diplomatic wrestling in the world arena was immediately reached and adhered to thereafter across the Strait. Although it was hard-pressed to reject requests by countries allied with Taipei to switch diplomatic relations, Beijing constrained itself from encouraging and accepting such a switch. In August 2008, the newly elected left-wing president of Paraguay intended to give up Taiwan and establish formal diplomatic relations with the mainland but was tactfully declined by Beijing. Henceforth, the "Paraguay model" for a cross-Strait "diplomatic truce" was followed by both sides in the similar cases of Malawi and Salvador.[25] In order to support the diplomatic truce and preserve cross-Strait stability, it is believed that the requests of some of Taipei's remaining allies to approach Beijing intending to switch their diplomatic recognition had been turned down by Beijing. The only exception was the Gambia, which unilaterally cut off its official relations with Taipei in November 2013. However, Beijing had avoided reestablishing diplomatic relations with the Gambia until March 2016, after the KMT had already been defeated by the DPP in the January presidential election.[26]

Compared with the diplomatic tug-of-war, which is primarily a bilateral arrangement, Beijing was more cautious about making any hasty concession allowing Taipei to join any highly symbolic international organization in an effort to expand Taiwan's "international space." Because such multilateral accommodations would be much more difficult, if not impossible, to be reversed, the scenario of two Chinas or one China, one Taiwan is quite likely to become a reality if the international space permitted by the mainland was to be taken advantage of by a pro-independence Taiwanese administration.

However, when then KMT chairman Wu Po-hsiung visited Beijing and raised again the question of Taiwan's international organization membership in May 2008, President Hu committed to addressing the concerns of the Taiwanese people in regard to security, dignity, and international space, with a priority given to discussing Taipei's wish to participate in the World Health Organization. On the eve of 2009, Hu advocated again to allow Taiwan's "reasonable" participation in global organizations based on the one-China principle, which thereafter was exemplified by permitting Taiwan to participate in the World Health Organization's implementation of the International Health Regulations under the name of "Contact Point in Taipei" on January 13, 2009.[27] After a series of negotiations, in May 2009, Taiwan was granted for the first time observer status and invited by the World Health Assembly (WHA) under the name of "Chinese Taipei" after a 38-year effort. The WHA model marked unprecedented progress in the long-standing and annoying disputes about the international space issue. Taiwan's attendance in the annual WHA went on for eight years until 2017, when the cross-Strait relationship descended again into a stalemate.

As widely expected, the WHA model had been applied to Taiwan's participation in more nongovernmental organizations (NGOs) and intergovernmental organizations of less political sensitivity, such as economic, social, and public health organizations. In September 2013, the director general of Taiwan's Civil Aeronautics Administration (CAA) was invited for the first time by the International Civil Aviation Organization (ICAO) to attend the ICAO Assembly as a "guest" under the name "Chinese Taipei CAA."

Based on the 1992 Consensus and cross-Strait consultation, Taiwan also participated in a number of regional and international organizations in different capacities. For instance, with the name "Separate Customs Territory of Taiwan, Penghu, Kinmen, and Matsu," Taipei acceded to the World Trade Organization's Government Procurement Agreement in 2009 and concluded Economic Partnership Agreements with Singapore and New Zealand – who are not Taipei's diplomatic allies – in 2013. Taiwan was also admitted to the South Pacific Regional Fisheries Management Organisation in 2012 and the North Pacific Fisheries Commission in 2015 as a fishing entity under the name "Chinese Taipei." Taipei also gained access to higher global visibility, usually with help from Beijing, including taking part in more international events in a pragmatic manner, like bidding for and hosting international games, such as the successful bidding for the 2017 Taipei Summer Universiade and the first 2019 Taichung East Asian Youth Games. As mentioned earlier, even though Beijing was constantly worried about any moves that might lend a sense of international legitimacy or symbols of statehood to Taipei, it still made attempts to raise Taipei's international profile and provide broader international space to Ma's administration that vowed to insist on the 1992 Consensus.

Third, there was an improvement in political interaction and an increase in mutual confidence. After the January 2008 election victory of the KMT, President Hu seized the "window of opportunity" to hold a meeting on April 12, 2008, with then-vice president-elect Vincent Siew as chairman of the Cross-Straits Common Market Foundation during the Bo'ao Forum.[28] On May 28, 2008, Hu met with then KMT chairman Wu Po-hsiung, the first meeting between the heads of the CPC and the KMT as ruling parties, and agreed to recommence semiofficial dialogue between the two sides.

In October 2013, right after the Xi-Siew meeting ahead of the Asia-Pacific Economic Cooperation (APEC) summit in Indonesia, Zhang Zhijun, minister of the Taiwan Affairs Office (TAO), exchanged brief pleasantries with his counterpart Wang Yu-chi, minister of the Mainland Affairs Council (MAC), addressing each other by their official titles for the first time.[29] On February 11, 2014, Zhang welcomed Wang in Nanjing, marking the first official, high-level contact between the two sides since 1949. Both sides agreed on initiating a direct and regular communication channel between the two institutes to facilitate cross-Strait engagement, and on establishing SEF and ARATS offices in their respective territories. Four months later, Zhang flew to Taiwan and became the first TAO minister to set foot on the island since 1949. On the eve of Tsai's inauguration, Taipei's justice minister Luo Ying-shay embarked on a five-day visit to Beijing in March 2016, making her the first justice minister from Taiwan to visit the mainland in her official capacity since 1949.

Cross-Strait political engagement ascended to its peak on November 7, 2015, when Xi and Ma shook hands in Singapore, addressing each other as "mister" within their capacity as "leader of Mainland China" and "leader of Taiwan," respectively, marking the first meeting between top leaders of both sides in 66 years since the end of Chinese Civil War in 1949. This historic meeting, as the culmination of mutual efforts to replace confrontation and conflict with dialogue and reconciliation, highlighted the political trust and delivered goodwill to maintain cross-Strait peace and development.

Fourth, this period also witnessed a surge in social and personnel exchanges. After millions of mainland Chinese soldiers and civilians left the mainland to Taiwan in 1949, cross-Strait isolation was finally broken when Taipei lifted travel restrictions for those with close relatives on the mainland in December 1987. The visit of the first group of Taiwan residents to reunite with their families on the mainland was remembered as a momentous occasion for the end of a 38-year-long severance and opened an opportunity for the development of social contact across the Strait, albeit with severe restraint and control. On June 13, 2008, the ARATS and the SEF signed documents agreeing that Taiwan would open to mainland tourists and allow entry of up to 3,000 visitors every day. As required by Taipei in the initial stage, mainland tourists must enter into, visit, and exit from Taiwan in groups. However, economically benefiting from the flood of mainland tourists, Taipei agreed in 2012 that tourists from Beijing, Shanghai, and Xiamen City could travel to Taiwan individually. Soon after that, the permission list was expanded to cover more mainland cities.[30]

On July 4, 2008, weekend charter flights began and carried the first mainland tourist group to Taiwan since 1949. The visit of Chen Yunlin, then chief of ARATS, to Taiwan in November 2008 marked the first-ever meeting between leaders of the ARATS and the SEF in Taiwan. During this visit, the two institutions signed four accords concerning direct transportation and food security. On December 15, 2008, direct shipping, air transport, and postal services were formally launched, signaling that the Three Links had finally become a reality after being put off for 30 years. The Agreement on Cross-Strait Air Traffic Supply reached on April 26, 2009, started regular passenger and cargo flights, and indicated the normalization of cross-Strait air transport service. From 2008 to 2015, direct flights between the two sides rose from 108 to 890 every week. With the full relaxation of restrictions on cross-Strait travel, the number of cross-Strait passenger exchanges doubled from 4.65 million in 2008 to 9.86 million in 2015. In 2016, 3.64 million mainland residents visited Taiwan, while Taiwan residents coming to the mainland rose to 5.74 million (Figure 2.3 and Table 2.3).[31]

The facilitation of travel regulations and implementation of direct flight brought forth the positive development of cultural, educational, religious, scientific, sporting, and media exchanges across the Strait.[32] Take media cooperation as an example. Beijing had opened up to central media and local media from Taipei in 1987 and 1996, respectively. It was only in 2001 and 2008 that central and local media from the mainland were allowed to open in Taiwan. However, in April 2005, the Xinhua News Agency and the *People's Daily*, two important mainland central media outlets, were suspended to report in Taiwan by Chen's administration. Despite this setback, cross-Strait media exchanges regained positive momentum after Ma took office. In July 2008,

Taipei allowed the Xinhua News Agency and the *People's Daily* to resume their operations in Taiwan and extended the period for mainland media reporters to be based in Taiwan from one month to three months. On November 1, 2008, the TAO issued new measures for Taiwanese journalists, including delegating approval authority and simplifying approval procedures, so as to provide convenience and assistance to Taiwanese journalists for mainland media coverage. These mutual efforts ensured that cross-Strait news exchanges and media cooperation were regularized again.

Fifth, there was a significant ice-breaking of security exchanges. In striking contrast with the flourishing economic cooperation and social exchanges, military tension and security apprehensions still lingered over the Strait. Driven by the urgent requirement of comprehensive peaceful development of cross-Strait relations, the two sides began to touch upon

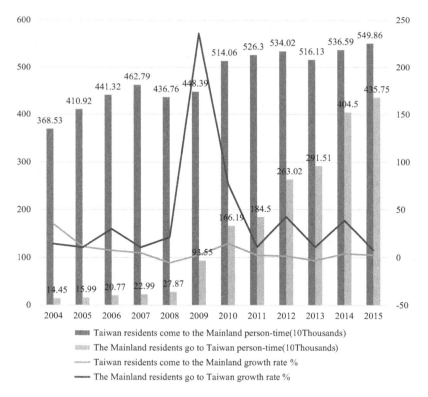

Figure 2.3 Cross-Strait personnel exchanges (2004–2015). (Note: Numbers represent 10,000 people.)

Table 2.3 Cross-Strait personnel exchanges (2004–2015)

Year	Taiwan residents coming to the mainland		Mainland residents going to Taiwan	
	Persons (ten thousands)	Growth rate %	Persons (ten thousands)	Growth rate %
2004	368.53	34.9	14.45	14.2
2005	410.92	11.45	15.99	10.58
2006	441.32	7.4	20.77	29.8
2007	462.79	4.86	22.99	10.7
2008	436.76	−5.6	27.87	21.2
2009	448.39	2.66	93.55	235.7
2010	514.06	14.65	166.19	77.64
2011	526.3	2.38	184.5	11.02
2012	534.02	1.47	263.02	42.56
2013	516.13	−3.31	291.51	10.86
2014	536.59	3.96	404.5	38.76
2015	549.86	2.47	435.75	7.72

Source: Sun Yafu, *40 Years of Cross-Straits Relations (1979–2019)* (Beijing: Jiuzhou Press, 2020), 323.

the military confidence-building measures (CBMs) issue, though fairly cautiously. Highlighting the removal of mainland missiles as the precondition, President Ma made a proposal on December 12, 2008, to develop cross-Strait talks on CBMs.[33] One month later, President Hu formally announced in December 2008 that the two sides should "end the history of confrontation" by signing a peace agreement, "engage in contacts and exchanges on military issues at a proper time," and explore the setting up of a military mutual trust mechanism in a bid to stabilize cross-Strait relations and ease concerns about military security.[34] It was the first time that Beijing had sent out such a clear message on this issue. In its 2009 National Defense Report, Taipei's Defense Ministry for the first time called for cross-Strait military CBMs that would reduce the chance of conflict in the Strait and lower the probability of accidental provocation of war.[35] The 2010 mainland China's Defense white paper endorsed Taipei's proposal by suggesting to conduct cross-Strait military exchanges aiming to establish CBMs. In the November 2012 report to the 18th CPC National Congress, Beijing recommitted to establishing mutual military trust mechanisms and reaching a peace accord between the two sides. Thereafter, Beijing and Taipei gradually stepped up security contacts and exchanges, including a series of maritime rescue joint exercises conducted by the coast guards from the two sides in the Strait since 2010. In November 2014, 21 Taiwanese army reserve generals visited Guangdong Province, which was the first time since 1949 that a group of Taiwanese reserve generals visited the mainland. Regrettably, the infant cross-Strait military exchanges had been subsequently rolled back because of the divergent political stance and differing security concerns between the two sides, in addition to the lack of consensus on the island.[36]

Rationale and achievement of Beijing's peaceful development policy

It is clear that Beijing's Taiwan policy has undergone a few rounds of evident and profound transitions in the past seven decades based on the ever-changing cross-Strait interactions and the trilateral Beijing–Taipei–Washington relations. The adoption and advocacy of peaceful development were undoubtedly one of the most important and successful transitions that had contributed to the eight-year peace and stability in the Strait. For Beijing, there were three vital reasons leading to these policy changes.

First, Beijing believed cross-Strait peaceful development is the best way to achieve peaceful reunification. Fulfilling national reunification is the persistent goal of the mainland for decades. The original idea of pursuing reunification through peace and development can be dated back to the 1950s. As early as May 26, 1955, Chairman Mao Zedong stated publicly that the "Taiwan issue can be resolved by negotiation" and "peace comes first" (*heping weishang*).[37] On January 30, 1956, Premier Zhou Enlai officially announced the new policy that "in addition to actively preparing for the liberation of Taiwan by force if necessary," Beijing "will try to liberate Taiwan peacefully."[38] The doctrine of "peaceful reunification" through the "one country, two systems" formula proposed by Deng Xiaoping has been succeeded and reaffirmed by Beijing, even though Beijing was forced to put "containing Taiwan independence" in a more prominent position when the cross-Strait relationship was thrown into a dangerous stalemate during Lee's and Chen's administrations.

For Beijing, the constant tension between the two sides would not only provide Taiwan's pro-independence wing with the opportunity to persuade more Taiwanese to stand with them out of fear and antagonism and incite anti-China populism but also put Beijing-friendly Taiwanese in an embarrassing position. On the contrary, a peaceful development policy from Beijing would cripple the momentum of Taiwan independence on the island, and help Beijing to reinforce the Taiwanese people's empathy and friendship in the mainland, as well as build confidence and faith in the prospect of peaceful reunification across the Strait.

Second, Beijing believed cross-Strait peaceful development to be conducive to its national modernization roadmap. From 1978 to 2008, the economic boom had positioned the mainland as the third biggest economy in the world in terms of gross domestic product (GDP), with an astonishingly average annual growth rate of 9.8%. Inspired by this great success, Beijing ambitiously announced in November 2002 that the years from 2000 to 2020 would be a "period of strategic opportunities" (*zhanlue jiyuqi*), and China would endeavor to fulfill fundamental modernization by 2020 and reach the level of medium developed countries by 2050.[39] In order to reach this goal, Beijing urgently needed a friendly and benign international environment, including a peaceful and stable cross-Strait situation, because of the high sensitivity and vulnerability associated with its rapid economic expansion in an age of globalization. In addition, aggravated domestic challenges, such as regional imbalances, social unfairness, the urban–rural gap, had also pushed Beijing to focus on internal challenges.[40] The reallocation of emphasis on national development and the new international political/economic reality after the Cold War had made China come to understand that its national interests in an interdependent world can be best served by positive international cooperation and coordination.[41] For Beijing, there was no reason to be involved in any unnecessary external disputes or conflicts, including the cross-Strait issue, which might deviate it from its modernization ambition.

Another driver motivating Beijing to go beyond a zero-sum calculation was its ever-growing confidence in its rising power status and the belief that "time is on its side." For example, in 1992, Taiwan's GDP was as high as about 45% of the mainland's when the two sides were preparing for the first Wang–Koo meeting. After just 16 years, however, the number had plunged to 9% in 2008 when Ma started his first term. By 2008, the total value of China's foreign trade had leapt to US$2562 billion, which was 124 times the value that it was in 1978. China's contribution to global economic growth was around 20% in 2008, making China one of the strongest engines and most influential players of the world economy.[42] For Beijing, on one hand, cross-Strait peaceful development would be helpful for its modernization goal; on the other hand, the continuous modernization progress of the mainland will correspondingly "determine the fundamental structure and developmental direction of cross-Strait relations."[43] In sum, the commencement of economic reform in 1979, the access to the WTO in 2001, and the consequential marvelous success achieved had not only opened a new stage of modern Chinese history but infused increasingly stronger dynamics to Beijing's Taiwan policy transition.

Third, Beijing believed cross-Strait peaceful development is the most feasible approach to accumulate mutual trust and win the hearts and minds of Taiwanese. After the cross-Strait isolation was broken in the late 1980s, flourishing trade and massive movement of personnel between both sides became a reality. For example, as of October 2008, the number of Taiwanese who had visited the mainland amounted to 50.7 million, while the number of mainland Chinese who had visited Taiwan had reached 1.85 million. In 1979, there was no cross-Strait investment at all and the trade was less than US$46 million. As of October 2008, the mainland had approved more than 77,000 projects from Taiwanese investors and the total value of cross-Strait trade had reached US$840 billion, among which exports from Taiwan to the mainland totaled about US$694.7 billion, reaching a surplus of US$546.4 from cross-Strait trade.[44] Since 1993, the mainland has been the most attractive destination for Taiwanese investment.[45] Since 2002, mainland China has supplanted the US as Taiwan's largest export market, as well as the largest origin of Taiwan's trade surplus, and its most important dependent market.

Undoubtedly, the relationship between mainland China and Taiwan had already become one of interdependence, characterized by a win–win pattern of mutual benefits. Nonetheless, the domestic political and social reality on Taiwan, signaled by Ma's declaration of the "Three No's"[46] and the preference among most Taiwanese toward maintaining the status quo, had reminded Beijing of the importance and necessity of winning the hearts and minds of Taiwanese. By advocating cross-Strait peaceful development in accordance with the principle of "placing the hope of reunification on Taiwan people," Beijing intended to promote social engagement, enhance economic integration, ease political and security tension, and accumulate mutual trust across the Strait, so as to allay the widespread suspicion and concerns among Taiwanese and thus create a public mood more favorable to the mainland.

After Ma Ying-jeou was sworn in to his presidency, cross-Strait exchanges and cooperation surged, with the cross-Strait relationship being described as the "best we've seen since 1949" by Ma in his meeting with Xi in Singapore.[47] There were indeed some impressive achievements made during this honeymoon period of cross-Strait relations.

To begin with, there had been a large expansion of engagement fields. By August 2015, 11 rounds of cross-Strait negotiations had produced 23 formal agreements, of which 21 have come into effect, along with 2 consensuses. With that, cross-Strait exchanges and cooperation, which had been mainly confined in economic and social fields for years, expanded into judicial, financial, diplomatic, and even the most sensitive military and political fields. For example, the signing of the judicial cooperation on April 26, 2009, and the mainland courts' recognition of verdicts in civil cases made by Taiwanese courts on May 14, 2009, had actually touched upon the sensitive topic of sovereignty and political coordination.[48] In echoing Ma's proposal to reach a peace agreement through negotiation, President Hu for the first time suggested on December 31, 2008, that both sides "start a discussion about political relations under the special condition before reunification in a pragmatic manner," which will lead to "a peace accord across the Strait."[49] That could and should be regarded as a milestone in mainland political policy adjustment in almost 60 years. In November 2012, Hu proposed again to explore and reach a "proper and reasonable arrangement" for the political relationship through mutual efforts. Concerned by the "longstanding political division between the two sides," President Xi restated in October 2013 that Beijing was "willing to engage in reciprocal negotiations on bilateral political issues with Taiwan under the 'one China' framework."[50]

Second, two-way exchanges were realized. Since the mainland opened its gates to the world in 1979, tourists, goods, and capital from Taiwan began to get access to the mainland and Taiwan was rewarded by numerous beneficiary treatments. However, it had been mainly a one-way road as Taipei imposed close confinement due to "national security concerns" for decades. The agreements about mainland tourists and the launching of cross-Strait regular passenger and cargo flights, as well as the consensus on encouraging mainland investment in Taiwan, however, changed the unidirectional channel into a two-way expressway. For instance, in 2000, only about 103,000 mainland residents visited Taiwan, while 311 million Taiwan residents came to the mainland. After Ma took office, Taiwan residents coming to the mainland rose steadily from 4.37 million in 2008 to 5.49 million in 2015, while mainland visitors to Taiwan rose sharply from nearly 279,000 to 4.36 million.[51] In 2009, annual investment from mainland enterprises in Taiwan amounted to US$37 million, visibly dwarfed by the US$1.88 billion of Taiwanese investment in the mainland. However, with the relaxation of restrictions by Taipei in June 2009, mainland companies' investment in the island consequently rose to US$247 million in 2015.[52] The longstanding one-way capital flow across the Strait had also been transformed.

Third, there was a clear evolution from sporadic and functional accords to a comprehensive agreement. Starting from the four accords reached by the first Wang–Koo meeting in 1993, all of the institutional arrangements across the Strait only targeted some specific issues, such as food security, agricultural exportation, charted flights, postal service, customs inspection, and investment protection. However, the astounding growth of economic, trade, and social links across the Strait made a comprehensive agreement framework an imperative for the two sides. In order to normalize and regulate cross-Strait exchanges, Beijing cooperated with Taipei's proposal of the ECFA, an all-round economic cooperation mechanism, aiming to institutionalize economic and trade cooperation, and accelerate the interdependence between the two sides. The signing of the ECFA pioneered a new wave of institution building and agreement negotiation across the Strait, including the CSSTA thereafter reached in 2013.

Fourth, was the formation of a multilayered structure of negotiation channels. The quasi-official interaction between the ARATS and the SEF used to be the only public platform since 1991 in dealing with cross-Strait issues. During Ma's administration, not only were institutionalized talks between the two institutes resumed after a nine-year hiatus, but multilevel channels have been employed to improve the speed and efficiency of negotiation. For example, civilian channels like the Cross-Strait Economic and Cultural Forum and the Cross-Strait Agricultural Cooperation Forum, and party-to-party channels like the CPC–KMT Forum and Strait Forum, a quasi-official channel like the Bo'ao Forum, and international channels like the unofficial summit of APEC were all launched. What is more important, high-level political communication mechanisms had been established. After the landmark Xi-Ma meeting, hailed as a milestone in cross-Strait relations, the two sides set up a ministerial-level hotline between the TAO and the MAC on December 30, 2015, and made the first conversation via the hotline on February 5, 2016, by Minister Zhang Zhijun, then chief of the TAO, and Minister Xia Liyan, then chief of the MAC. Through all of these multilayered structures of communication between the leadership of the two sides, ideas can be shared, concerns can be addressed, high-level confidence can be built, and resolutions can be reached more easily.

Conclusion

Since May 20, 2008, cross-Strait ties have taken a historic upturn and achieved notable progress. The interlinked policies and proposals advocated by the mainland during Ma's administration demonstrated a new roadmap of its Taiwan policy after antagonistic wrangling with Lee Teng-hui and Chen Shuibian. Beijing believed and expected that following the order of "economics before politics" and "easy issues before difficult issues," the spillover effect of economic cooperation and social engagement could help bridge the political and ideological gulf between the two sides and transcend their antagonistic morass. Indeed, Beijing had established a peaceful development framework featuring comprehensive rapprochement ever since 2008 in order to lay down a stable foundation for mutually beneficial economic cooperation as well as political, diplomatic, and military détente across the Strait, which will be essential for the attainment of peaceful reunification.

Nonetheless, the decrease of tension and increase of cooperation since 2008 had not led to results desired by Beijing. Hovering over the eight-year flourishing cross-Strait exchanges and cooperation that had made much headway was the deep-rooted distrust and suspicion among the Taiwanese. The dissenting voices made by independence-leaning forces also cast a haunting shadow over cross-Strait relations and the prospect of national reunification.[53] Undoubtedly, what had happened on the island after eight years of peaceful development ran counter to Beijing's policy goals and expectations. The economic interdependence and social integration across the Strait had neither drawn Taiwan closer to the mainland nor led to political identification and psychological intimacy.[54] Instead, concerns were raised that Ma's administration had made Taiwan's economy overly dependent on the mainland and left Taipei vulnerable to political pressure from Beijing, contributing to the soaring public support of Tsai.

At the same time, anti-mainland public sentiment on Taiwan, reflected by the massive Sunflower protest movement in 2014, had continued to grow, evaporating the Chinese identity foundation for unification. Even worse, with increasing numbers of Taiwanese youth saying they don't consider themselves to be Chinese, Taiwan had become more distant from mainland China, and this consequently made it harder, instead of easier, for the mainland to charm the public into favoring Beijing's ultimate goal of peacefully unifying the two sides. Following the visible victory of the DPP in the 2016 election and the inauguration of Tsai Ing-wen, the period that was broadly viewed as peaceful development had come to an end. Henceforth, the cross-Strait relationship chartered into turbulent waters once again.

Notes

1 On April 29, 2008, President Hu Jintao proposed the "16-character guideline" of "building mutual trust, putting aside disputes, seeking common ground while reserving differences, and creating a win-win situation" when he met with the honorary chairman of the KMT, Lien Chan, regarding the historical legacy and future situation of cross-Strait relations. See "Hu Jintao and Lien Chan Talks on Cross-Strait Relations Put Forward Four-Point Proposal," The Central People's Government of PRC, April 29, 2008, http://www.gov.cn/ldhd/2005-04/29/content_9780.htm.
2 Zhou Zhihuai, "Mainland's Taiwan Policy and New Developments in Cross-Strait Relations," *Taiwan Studies*, no. 1 (2006), 2.
3 The political coalition led by the KMT is called the "Pan-Blue Camp" or the "Blue Camp" for short, because the KMT's flag is blue. The alignment led by the DPP is called the "Pan-Green Camp" or the "Green Camp" for short, because the DPP's flag is green.
4 "CPC, KMT Work for Formal End of Cross-Straits Hostility," Xinhua News Agency, April 29, 2005, http://www.chinadaily.com.cn/english/doc/2005-04/29/content_438686.htm.
5 "Communiqué of Hu-Lien Conference," Xinhua News Agency, March 20, 2006, http://tga.mofcom.gov.cn/article/ls/shwz/200603/20060301716256.shtml.
6 "People First Party Declared 6 Consensus Reached by 'Hu-Soong Conference,'" Sina News, May 12, 2005, http://news.sina.com.cn/c/2005-05-12/17406624798.shtml.

 7 "Hu Jintao Meets Lien Chan and Other Taiwanese Attending Cross-Strait Economic and Trade Forum," Taiwan Affairs Office of the State Council of PRC, April 16, 2006, http://www.gwytb.gov.cn/zt/hu/201101/t20110123 _1723853.htm.

 8 Hu Jintao, "Report at the Seventeenth National Congress of the CPC," The State Council Information Office of PRC, October 24, 2017, http://www.scio.gov.cn /37231/Document/1566887/1566887.htm.

 9 Charter flights would be arranged for during Qingming Festival, the Dragon Boat Festival, and the Mid-Autumn Festival, in addition to the Chinese Lunar New Year season. The two sides also agreed to open charter flights for emergent medical rescue, first aid for the handicapped, and charter cargo flights for special needs. See "Cross-Strait Holiday Plane Arrangement Will be Expanded to Qingming and Other Four Traditional Festivals," The Central People's Government of PRC, June 14, 2006, http://www.gov.cn/jrzg/2006-06/14/con-tent_309499.htm.

10 "Chen Shui-bian Says Cross-Strait Charter Flights and Open Travel to Taiwan Should be Implemented As Soon As Possible," *Xinlang News*, February 26, 2007, http://news.sina.com.cn/c/2007-02-26/130812373679.shtml.

11 However, because of the tension across the Strait, hardly any mainland tourist groups visited Taiwan before Ma took office.

12 "Press Conference on May 31, 2006," Taiwan Affairs Office of the State Council of PRC, May 31, 2006, http://www.scio.gov.cn/xwfbh/gbwxwfbh/xwfbh/gtb/Document/314408/314408.htm.

13 Hu Jintao, "Addresses Commemorating the 30th Anniversary of the Issuance of Message to Compatriots in Taiwan," Xinhua News Agency, December 31, 2008, http://www.gov.cn/ldhd/2008-12/31/content_1193074.htm.

14 Hu Jintao, "Addresses Commemorating the 30th Anniversary."

15 "Historic Taiwan-China Trade Deal Takes Effect," BBC, September 12, 2010, https://www.bbc.com/news/world-asia-pacific-11275274.

16 Huang Yanping and Deng Lijuan, "Research on the Development of Economic Cooperation between China Mainland and Taiwan: 2008–2013," *Asia-Pacific Economy Review*, no. 6 (2014), 130–135.

17 Shi Zhengfang, "Cross-Strait Economic Integration and Development: Concept Definition and Path Selection," *Taiwan Research Journal*, no. 3 (2021), 41–49.

18 "Premier Li Promotes Cross-Strait Economic Cooperation," The State Council of PRC, April 10, 2014, http://english.www.gov.cn/premier/news/2014/08/23/content_281474983010904.htm.

19 "Wang Yi Declared 10 Preferential Policies toward Taiwan Facing International Financial Crisis," December 21, 2008, http://www.gwytb.gov.cn/zyjh/zyjh0.asp?zyjh_m_id=1674.

20 However, China Mobile announced in April 2013 that it had to terminate the agreement to buy a stake of Far EasTone because of Taiwan's regulatory hurdles.

21 Yang Yuntao, "Taiwan's Fubon Financial Company to Increase Xiamen Bank Stake," *China Daily*, July 21, 2009.

22 Li Xiaoxiao and Chen Zitao, "Research on the Impact of Preferential Policies on Taiwanese Investment in the Mainland," *Taiwan Studies*, no. 5 (2021), 56–63.

23 Hu Jintao, "Report at the Seventeenth National Congress of the CPC."

24 Hu Jintao, "Addresses Commemorating the 30th Anniversary."

25 It was reported that Salvador, just like Paraguay, had extended its will to switch formal diplomatic relations from Taiwan to the mainland. However, the mainland

has constrained itself from doing so. Malawi's case demonstrated exactly the tacit understanding as an opposite example, that is, Taiwan refused the request of Malawi to resume formal diplomacy in early 2009, after Malawi changed its position to the mainland in January 2008.

26 Xiu Chunping, "A Study of Ma Ying-jeou' 'Flexible Diplomacy,'" *Taiwan Studies*, no. 4 (2012), 44–48.
27 "WHO Agrees to Include Taiwan in the Implementation of IHR," Taiwan Centers for Disease Control, January 23, 2009, https://www.cdc.gov.tw/En/Bulletin/Detail/ijDOgFLf8UnPhkPCa7yYeg?typeid=158.
28 "Hu Jintao Meets Vincent Siew; They Exchanged Opinions on Cross-Strait Economic Exchange and Co-Operation," Xinhua News Agency, April 12, 2008, https://china.huanqiu.com/article/9CaKrnJkn4Y.
29 Wang addressed Zhang as "Minister Zhang" and Zhang addressed Wang as "Minister Wang." Before that, President Xi and Vincent Siew, who stepped down from the position of Taiwan's vice president in May 2012, just finished a closed-door talk.
30 By the end of 2012, individual tourists from the mainland cities of Chengdu, Chongqing, Nanjing, Hangzhou, Guangzhou, Tianjin, Fuzhou, Ji'nan, and Xi'an were allowed to visit Taiwan.
31 Sun Yafu and Li Peng, *40 Years of Cross-Straits Relations (1979–2019)* (Beijing: Jiuzhou Press, 2020), 322.
32 Yafu and Peng, *40 Years of Cross-Straits Relations*, 324–337.
33 Ma Ying-jeou, "Peace Plan: China and Taiwan," *Washington Post*, December 12, 2008.
34 Hu Jintao, "Addresses Commemorating the 30th Anniversary."
35 ROC Ministry of National Defense, *2009 National Defense Report* (Taipei: Ministry of National Defense, 2009), Chapter 8.
36 Bonnie Glaser, "Building Trust Across the Taiwan Strait: A Role for Military Confidence-Building *Measures*," CSIS Report, January 12, 2010, https://www.csis.org/analysis/building-trust-across-taiwan-strait.
37 Mao Zedong, *Selected Works of Mao Zedong's Statements upon Diplomacy* (Beijing: Zhongyang Wenxian Press, 1994), 211.
38 Zhou Enlai, "Government Report to the 2nd National Congress of the Chinese People's Political Consultative Conference," January 30, 1956, http://www.chinataiwan.org/wxzl/zhyyl/zhel/200211/t20021112_86833.htm.
39 Jiang Zemin, "Report at the 16th National Congress of the CPC," CPC, November 8, 2002, http://cpc.people.com.cn/GB/64162/64168/64569/65444/4429125.html.
40 Hu Angang, *Prospect for China's Development* (Hangzhou: Zhejiang People Press, 1999).
41 Hu Jintao, "Report at the Seventeenth National Congress of the CPC."
42 "China's Economic Contribution Was No.1 in 2008," January 3, 2009, http://news.sina.com.cn/c/2009-01-23/034015076267s.shtml.
43 "Hu Jintao Emphasizes to Hold Tightly the Theme of Peaceful Development in Cross-Strait Relations," The Central People's Government of PRC, March 4, 2008, http://www.gov.cn/test/2008-06/13/content_1015459.htm.
44 Wang Yi, "Prospects of Peaceful Development in Cross-Strait Relations," December 31, 2008, https://www.mfa.gov.cn/ce/cgsf//chn/zhuanti/twwt/dtxw/t529943.htm.
45 "China Most Popular Spot for Taiwan Investors: MOEA," *Taiwan Economic News*, March 12, 2002.

46 In his inauguration speech on May 20, 2008, Ma announced that his cross-Strait policy was "no unification, no independence and no use of force." See Ma Ying-Jeou, "Inaugural Address," May 20, 2008, https://china.usc.edu/ma-ying-jeou-%E2%80%9Cinaugural-address%E2%80%9D-may-20-2008.

47 Philip Wen, "China and Taiwan A 'Family', Says Xi Jinping at Historic Meeting of Leaders," *The Sidney Morning Herald*, November 8, 2015, https://www.smh.com.au/world/china-and-taiwan-a-family-says-xi-jinping-at-historic-meeting-of-leaders-20151107-gktf07.html.

48 "Mainland Further Facilitates Recognition of Taiwan Court Decisions," May 14, 2009, http://www.chinaconsulatechicago.org/eng/zt/taiwanissue/200905/t20090514_5424953.htm; "ARATS, SEF Sign Agreements on Regular Flights, Financial, Judicial Co-Op," *People's Daily*, April 26, 2009, http://en.people.cn/90001/90776/90785/6645252.html.

49 Hu Jintao, "Addresses Commemorating the 30th Anniversary."

50 Chris Wang, "Political Division Must Be Resolved: Xi Jinping," *Taipei Times*, October 7, 2013, https://www.taipeitimes.com/News/front/archives/2013/10/07/2003573898.

51 Yafu and Peng, *40 Years of Cross-Straits Relations*, 322.

52 Ministry of the Commerce of PRC, Taiwan, Hong Kong and Macao Department, The Statistics of Mainland-Taiwan Trade and Economic Cooperation, 2020, http://tga.mofcom.gov.cn/article/sjzl/taiwan.

53 Steve Goldstein, *China and Taiwan* (Cambridge, UK: Polity Press, 2015).

54 Shirley Lin, *Taiwan's China Dilemma* (Stanford, CA: Stanford University Press, 2016).

3 Selective engagement

Mainland China's dual-track Taiwan policy (2016–)

Introduction

In January 2016, Tsai Ing-wen was elected with 56% of the vote in the presidential campaign of Taiwan, beating her opponent Eric Chu by a margin of 25.04%. Meanwhile, the Democratic Progress Party (DPP) enjoyed a majority in the Legislative Yuan for the first time in history. The landslide victory of the DPP over the Kuomintang (KMT) made it the dominant party with both executive and legislative power in hand. Tsai won the campaign on the promise that she has the capability to develop Taiwan's stagnant economy, reduce social tensions, and maintain the status quo across the Taiwan Strait.[1] However, the repudiation of Tsai's administration of the one-China principle insisted by Beijing has ignited an intensifying pressure campaign from mainland China, driving cross-Strait relations into a deadlock after the eight-year energetic interaction and cooperative development during the Ma Ying-jeou administration.[2] Facing uncompromising countermeasures from Taipei and an enduring cross-Strait impasse, Beijing gradually forged a dual-track Taiwan policy framework featuring "selective engagement" after a short-term observation since the inauguration of Tsai in May 2016. This framework was continued and strengthened after Tsai skippered the DPP and won the 2020 presidential reelection with an increased share of the vote by appealing to "anti-China" sentiment.

Beijing's current selective engagement policy, which also can be characterized as sort of "congagement" policy, is a combination of both containment and engagement measures. It is perceived as a set of complementary dual-track approaches from two dimensions. First, in terms of the issue areas of the selective engagement policy, it is a combination of confrontational measures in security, political, and diplomatic fields, with coordinative approaches on economic, social, and cultural affairs. Second, in terms of the counterparts, it is a combination of spot-on punitive measures against the acute "Taiwan independence" firebrands of the green camp represented

DOI: 10.4324/9781003163275-3

by the DPP, with accommodative approaches toward all the other camps, covering a wide political spectrum ranging from the traditional blue camp represented by the KMT that sticks to the 1992 Consensus, to the "middle force" or the "White Force" (*baise liliang*) represented by Taipei City Mayor Ko Wen-je, who has suggested that "the two sides of the Taiwan Strait are one family." The strategic purpose of Beijing is to provide the necessary dynamics to maintain the economic and social cooperation momentum across the Strait and win the hearts and minds of the Taiwanese, while imposing sufficient pressure to deter the Tsai administration and the "deepgreen camp" activists from pursuing the radical pro-independence agenda.[3]

Track of containment in high-political areas

For Beijing, agreement or disagreement with the one-China principle is always the fundamental influential factor for the stability or turbulence of cross-Strait relations. After long-term difficult negotiations, Beijing and Taipei constructively reached a consensus about the one-China principle in 1992 – which was creatively termed by Dr. Su Chi as a somewhat ambiguous "1992 Consensus" in 2000 – and held the historical Wang–Koo meeting in April 1993. After a decade of tension across the Taiwan Strait during the Lee Teng-hui and Chen Shuibian administrations, the two sides began to enjoy an unprecedented period of peace and cooperation based on the 1992 Consensus after the KMT returned to power in 2008. Before the 2016 presidential campaign in Taiwan, as it was widely believed that the DPP would win the election, Beijing had repeatedly affirmed its insistence on the one-China principle as the "foundation and precondition" for positive interaction across the Strait and warned the DPP that "when the foundation is not stable, the earth moves and the mountains shake" (*jichu bulao, didong shanyao*).[4]

However, Beijing's warning was not taken seriously enough by the DPP leadership. Tsai publicly alleged before the 2016 election that, provided the DPP could win the campaign without major issues, Beijing would have no choice but to face the reality and "cuddle up itself to Taipei" (*zidong kaoguolai*).[5] She had also promised to her constituents that she would and could maintain the status quo during her presidency. Unfortunately, it seems that the Tsai administration has overestimated its capability to achieve that at its will, while underestimating Beijing's determination to defend the one-China principle even at a heavy cost to the cross-Strait relations. The reference that Taipei will conduct cross-Strait affairs in accordance with the Republic of China Constitution as well the Act Governing Relations Between the People of Taiwan Area and the Mainland Area (*liang'an renmin guanxi tiaoli*) in Tsai's inaugural speech on May 20, 2016, was regarded as an allusion to the acknowledgement of the one-China principle. Taking the necessity of Taiwan's electoral politics into consideration, Beijing's remark of "an unfinished exam paper" (*meiyou wancheng de dajuan*) left a window open for a transitional wait and see period.[6] It implied that Beijing would like to give the Tsai administration a period of time to pragmatically adjust DPP's pro-independence stance and clearly accept the one-China principle when there was no more campaign pressure. After her 2016 inauguration, Tsai advocated some new discourse, such as the "historical fact of 1992 meeting," "1992 common cognition," "New Four No's," and "Three New Ideas," aiming to win the trust of Beijing and ease the tension across the Strait.[7]

However, these efforts were nullified by some other contradictory behaviors of Taipei. For example, in her open letter marking DPP's 30th anniversary in September 2016, Tsai called on the party members to "resist pressure from China."[8] On October 4, 2016, Tsai told the *Wall Street Journal* that Beijing must face the reality that "Taiwan is a sovereignty independent state."[9] On May 18, 2017, Zhang Xiaoyue, the chief of the Mainland Affairs Council (MAC), criticized Beijing for ignoring the fact that Taiwan is "a sovereignty independent state," and there is "no possibility" for Taiwan to accept the one-China principle.[10] Premier Lai Ching-te, then leader of Taiwan's Executive Yuan (*xingzheng yuan*), announced on September 26, 2017, that he is "a politician who supports Taiwan independence."[11] On January 15, 2020, Tsai alleged four days after her reelection, "We are an independent country already and we call ourselves the Republic of China, Taiwan."[12]

At the same time, the Tsai administration is domestically endeavoring to pursue and promote the de-Sinicization (*qu zhongguo hua*) agenda ranging from social to cultural to educational fields.[13] For instance, Beijing was very upset when the High School Curriculum Review Commission under the Tsai administration decided to block the implementation of KMT-proposed curriculum amendments and stop teaching Chinese history as an independent course but as a part of the East Asian history curriculum.[14] The sweeping "Transitional Justice" (*zhuanxing zhengyi*) campaign initiated by the DPP to "strip the legitimacy of authoritarian rule" of the KMT also alerted Beijing. The behaviors of the DPP administration, including the removal and disposal of the signs and symbols related to Chiang Kai-shek, the political liquidation of KMT rule between 1945 and 1992, and commemoration of Japanese colonialism, are regarded as a part of the process to diminish the historical and legal bonds between the mainland and Taiwan by demonizing and delegitimizing the KMT government as an "alien authority" or a "foreign regime" (*wailai zhengquan*) forcibly imposed on Taiwan. In addition, the closer interaction between Taipei and Washington, as well as between

Taipei and Tokyo, highlighted by the unprecedented Trump–Tsai phone call in December 2016, dramatically deepened Beijing's distrust toward Tsai.[15]

Taken together, all of these behaviors made Beijing, which is historically always suspicious of the consistent pro-independence inclination of DPP politicians, reach the conclusion that there is little hope that the DPP would give up its "One Side, One State" (*yibian yiguo*) position and turn to endorse the principle that "both the mainland and Taiwan belong to one China." As a result, Beijing decided to take multidimensional confrontational measures in "high-political" areas, ranging from security to political to diplomatic areas, to contain the Tsai administration from pursuing the Taiwan-independence course. Not surprisingly, the tit-for-tat actions between the two sides drove the already tense cross-Strait relations into a downward spiral.

First, an environment of increased security dilemma and military standoff can be seen. Preparing to fight and defend "national sovereignty and territorial integrity" has always been the foremost obligation of the People's Liberation Army (PLA). In order to ensure the reunification of Taiwan, which is defined as an "unshakable historic task" (*shizhi buyu de lishi shiming*) by Beijing, the mainland has never ruled out the use of force and "reserve the option to use all necessary measures" to prevent Taiwan independence.[16] Keeping the Taiwan independence scenario in mind, the PLA is required to develop the capability to fight a war and win a war (*neng dazhang, da shengzhang*) under a more efficient commanding structure and combating system based on the comprehensive military reform initiated in November 2015. Driven by the concern that the Taiwanese administration might pursue de jure independence and supported by mainland China's continuous military budget increase as well the breakthrough in industrial–scientific–technological infrastructure, the PLA has commissioned a series of advanced weapon systems capable of anti-access/area denial operation and regional power projection in the West Pacific area in the past decade.[17] As warned by President Xi, the mainland is resolved to oppose "any separatist activity" and will "never allow anyone, any organization, or any political party, at any time or in any form" to separate Taiwan from China.[18]

In sharp contrast with the rather prudent and restrained employment of military leverage during the Ma administration, the PLA started to strengthen its military pressure upon Taipei in order to deter the growing Taiwan independence momentum. For example, in November 2016, PLA Air Force (PLAAF) airplanes made their first circumnavigation around Taiwan. Subsequently, more complex and sophisticated aircraft formations composed of H-6K strategic bombers, jet fighters, early warning airplanes, and electronic warfare airplanes of the PLA conducted "island encircling exercises" many times during their regular flight exercises beyond the First

Island Chain in the West Pacific Ocean. Echoing the Trump–Tsai call, the *Liaoning* aircraft carrier of the PLA Navy (PLAN) carried out its maiden circling patrol around the Taiwan island after conducting a far-sea drill in January 2017. In April 2018, the PLAN conducted a live-fire exercise into the Taiwan Strait after an unprecedented naval parade in the South China Sea. It was reported that on March 31, 2019, two PLAAF J-11 jets broke "the long-held tacit agreement" by crossing the median line of the Taiwan Strait, forcing the Taiwan Air Force to scramble several jets to intercept the aircraft, consequently igniting a ten-minute standoff between Taiwan and mainland warplanes. This was reportedly the first time that PLA warplanes intentionally crossed the median line, an informal but largely respected border of control for the two sides, since 1999.[19] On September 17, 2020, US Under Secretary of State Keith Krach arrived at Taipei for a three-day visit, the highest-ranking State Department official to visit Taiwan since 1979, which was regarded by Beijing as a blunt breach of US commitment to the framework of unofficial US–Taiwan relations. Right after the visit, the PLAAF dispatched a total of 37 aircraft (a mixture of H-6 bombers; J-10, J-11, and J-16 fighters; and a Y-8 antisubmarine warfare plane) and crossed the median line of the Taiwan Strait in two days. Beijing for the first time publicly denied the existence of a median line on September 21, 2020.[20]

By the same token, in responding to the large-scale naval exercise of the US in early October, the upgraded version of the "Two States Thesis" remarks made by Tsai in her October 10 speech, as well as the first formal confirmation of US troop presence on Taiwan on October 28, 2021, the PLA dramatically intensified military pressure by increasing the scale and composition of exercises. On the last day of October 2021, eight PLA aircraft, including one Y-8 anti-submarine warfare aircraft, six J-16 fighter jets, and one KJ-500 early warning aircraft, entered Taipei's self-proclaimed southwest air defense identification zone (ADIZ), with the Y-8 anti-submarine warfare aircraft also flying southeast of the island through the Bashi Channel. On the same day, two Y-9 patrol aircraft and one Y-9 reconnaissance aircraft flew through the Miyako Strait from the East China Sea into the Pacific Ocean east to the island of Taiwan, before returning via the same routes. These behaviors on the last day of the month brought the tally of PLA aircraft activity in the aerial area near Taiwan for exercises to approximately 196 in October. During those drills aiming to "deter Taiwan secessionist provocations" and "foreign interference attempts," the PLA broke the record on several occasions, namely the record-breaking 38 aircraft on October 1, 39 on October 2, and 56 on October 4. In addition, it was reported that a Mi-17 cargo helicopter and a WZ-10 attack helicopter were dispatched for the first time to the region and practiced multidimensional amphibious assaults and landings on October 26, 2021.[21] Nowadays, flying into Taipei's ADIZ has become a new normal while the PLA continues to expand its training and exercise routines beyond mainland China's coastal areas into the open seas. There is no doubt that those exercises and operations were aimed at sending the signal of deterrence to Taipei.

On the other hand, in the face of the rapid development of military power of the PLA, the Tsai administration formulated a new military strategy in March 2017 featuring "solid defense and multilayered deterrence" (*fangwei gushou, chongceng hezu*). Feng Shikuan, the then defense minister of Taipei, stated publicly that the army might "launch offensive attack" in order to "crash the enemy on the other side of the Strait."[22] After an increase of 3% in the 2018 defense budget (about US$11 billion), the Tsai administration proposed a 5.6% increase for the 2019 defense budget, increasing it from 327 billion New Taiwan dollars (NT$) to 346 billion. In 2021, the military budget was set to NT$453 billion, estimated to be 2.4% of GDP, representing a 4.4% increase over 2020.[23] Taipei is also determined to invest extensive resources into the indigenous manufacturing of advanced weapon systems, including submarines, fighter jets, missiles, and air-defense systems. As a result of Taipei's defensive self-sufficiency endeavors, the T-5 Brave Eagle indigenous jet trainer conducted its first test flight in June 2020, the first domestically manufactured rapid mine-laying ship was delivered in August 2020, construction of an indigenous diesel submarine was initiated in November 2020, and the first indigenous amphibious transport dock was launched in April 2021.[24]

Amid concerns that Taiwan's military would be no match for the PLA in terms of combat capability, Taipei has repeatedly pledged that the military will develop asymmetric warfare, procure new weapon systems, and reform its reserve force system to counter the growing pressure from the PLA. For example, in response to the report issued by the Pentagon claiming the PLA has set the goal of "developing the capabilities to counter the U.S. military in the Indo-Pacific region and compel Taiwan's leadership to the negotiation table on Beijing's terms" by 2027,[25] Taiwan's defense minister Chiu Kuo-cheng reaffirmed on November 5, 2021, the military's stance that the mainland "cannot force us to do anything" using non-peaceful means, and the armed forces will do everything it can to defend the island.[26] About one week later, while Tsai admitted at the National Day celebrations that Taiwan was facing the "most complex situation" in the past 72 years, she stressed "there should be absolutely no illusions that the Taiwanese people will bow to pressure" and Taipei will "continue to bolster our national defense and demonstrate our determination to defend ourselves."[27]

In addition to calling on the US to deepen bilateral military cooperation and strengthen bilateral intelligence exchanges, Taipei is also urging Washington to sell advanced weapon systems and key technologies to strengthen Taiwan's self-defense capability. In order to outcompete China amid the intensifying US–China rivalry, the Trump administration also drastically strengthened US–Taiwan security cooperation, highlighted by successive and massive arms sales to Taiwan.[28] By accusing Beijing of ramping up tensions in the Strait and aggressively attempting to alter the status quo, President Trump announced a series of ten arms sales packages during his four-year tenure, including one in 2017, one in 2018, three in 2019, and five in 2020. These arms sales significantly surpassed any of his predecessors over the past 40 years both in quantitative and qualitative terms.[29]

Currently, Taiwan's air force, through a US$3.68 billion project, is retrofitting its 144 F-16 A/B jets to F-16V, an upgraded version equipped with more advanced radar, and sophisticated combat and strike systems from the US. Additionally, in March 2019, Taipei submitted an official purchase request to the US for a fleet of F-16V fighter jets at a cost of NT$390 billion (about US$12.6 billion), which would include missiles and related logistics and the training of pilots and maintenance personnel.[30] President Trump approved the sale of 66 new F-16V fighters in August 2019, signaling a breakthrough in selling star jet fighters in 28 years since 1992. On November 18, 2021, Tsai commissioned into service 64 upgraded F-16V fighter jets, the most technologically advanced version of the storied multirole fighter jet, and commented this upgrade project showed the strength of Taiwan's cooperation with the US defense industry and represented "the steadfast promise of the Taiwan–U.S. partnership."[31]

More notably, the US arms sales model to Taiwan had also been considerably changed into a case-by-case model based on "allied states' needs" by normalizing the arms sales, simplifying the decision-making process, and promoting commercial sales in addition to official sales for sensitive weapon systems, as well as selling standard offensive weapons, such as 135 AGM-84H (SLAM-ER) air-launched cruise missiles, 11 HIMARS M142 Launchers (including 64 Army Tactical Missile Systems and 6 MS-110 Multispectral Airborne Reconnaissance Systems), 400 RGM-84L Harpoon Coastal Defense Systems, and 100 Launcher Transporter Units.[32] After a decade of arduous lobbying from Taipei, the Trump administration approved in April 2018 the marketing license needed for US manufacturers to sell US-made submarine technology that would enable Taiwan to build domestically designed and produced diesel-electric submarines, which is widely recognized as an offensive weapon and a pillar for "asymmetrical combat capability."[33] On November 16, 2021, the Taiwan Navy held a keel-laying ceremony of an indigenously developed submarine prototype, marking the end of the vessel's initial construction phase.

Following Trump's step, President Biden reiterated the US's "rock solid" commitment to Taiwan security and approved the first arms sale in August

2021, a deal of 40 new M109 self-propelled howitzers and associated equipment worth up to $750 million, just seven months after his inauguration.[34] A series of military acquisitions from the US equipped Taipei with more sophisticated and integrated capability for both defensive and offensive combat. Correspondingly, this inflamed Beijing's anxiety and impelled the PLA to maintain military preparedness.

Second, the extension of political impasses continued. Based on the 1992 Consensus, Beijing and Taipei established multilevel institutional mechanisms for communication and negotiation during the Ma administration, which were essential for mutual trust building across the Taiwan Strait. After Tsai took power, Beijing shut down all direct and regular official communication channels and platforms. For example, the institutional communication between Beijing's TAO and Taipei's MAC, the only official channel between the two sides, was closed down on May 20, 2016, the inauguration day of Tsai's first term. Simultaneously, the negotiation mechanism between the ARATS and the SEF, which had operated effectively for eight years, was suspended. Nowadays, all of the official and semiofficial communication mechanisms have come to an indefinite halt given Beijing's adamant insistence of recognition of the one-China principle versus Taipei's irreconcilable rejection of it.[35]

Tensions between the two sides have been inadvertently heightened because of the absence of an effective and institutional communication channel. For example, in January 2018, Beijing decided to unilaterally launch the south-to-north operation of the heavily trafficked M503 air route through the Taiwan Strait, and the extension of the W121, W122, and W123 feeder routes from cities on the mainland coast. In January 2015, Beijing proposed the initiation of the M503 flight route, approved by the International Civil Aviation Organization as a two-way route, to ease the crowded airspace and facilitate air travel. However, the proposal was opposed by the Ma administration since the routes were close to Taiwan's ADIZ. To appease Ma, Beijing specifically suspended the plan until the two sides reached a compromise through a two-month consultation. Previously, Beijing agreed to launch only southbound flights on route M503, put on hold three connecting lines, and moved the route six nautical miles closer to the Mainland. Since the first flight took off on the M503 flight route in March 2015, Beijing, although frustrated by the air traffic congestion, maintained the arrangement for several years just because of Taipei's complaint. In the face of Beijing's unilateral change without "prior consultation" with Taipei as before, the Tsai administration severely protested that was a break of the 2015 compromise and urged Beijing to sit down for a formal consultation. Unsurprisingly, such a demand was ignored by Beijing because of the lack of "political base for consultation," in other words, the acceptance of the one-China principle by Taipei.[36] In retaliation for not being consulted, the Tsai administration refused to approve the mainland airlines' application for additional Spring Festival charter flights, leading to the cancellation of 176 cross-Strait charter flights ahead of the Lunar New Year festival. As a result, 50,000 Taiwanese living and working on the mainland were stranded and had to find other ways to go back to Taiwan for family reunions.

After the outbreak of the COVID-19 pandemic in Wuhan City in January 2020, where a few hundred Taiwanese businesspeople and their family members lived, the lack of an official communications channel made the negotiation of a Taiwan-bound charter flight tense and difficult. After the first charter flight operated with 247 passengers on February 4, 2020, it took more than one month for the two sides to solve the disputes over quarantine measures, boarding lists, and for the airlines to carry out the evacuations.[37] During negotiations, the two sides pointed fingers at each other, as Taipei accused Beijing of not agreeing with its "priority" passenger lists and not carrying out necessary quarantine measures, while Beijing blamed Taipei for "using all kinds of excuses to obstruct and delay" flights and not allowing stranded Taiwanese to return home.[38] It is another example of how strained political relations led to inefficient cross-Strait communication and interruption of necessary cooperation even in the face of a deadly virus.

Third is the resurgence of "international space competition." Ever since 1949, the tug-of-war in the global arena for international space between Beijing and Taipei has never stopped except for a temporarily freeze when the two sides reached a tacit and unofficial diplomatic truce after Ma came into power in 2008. However, half a year after Tsai's inauguration, the diplomatic truce crumbled when Beijing began to make concerted and multifrontier efforts to squeeze the international space of Taipei to display its discontent with Tsai's consistent denial of the one-China principle.

The first frontier is the "diplomatic allies' competition." The termination of São Tomé and Príncipe's diplomatic relation with Taipei in December 2016, and the prompt establishment of official ties between the former and the People's Republic of China (PRC) five days later sent the first signal of the abandonment of the eight-year-long diplomatic truce. On June 13, 2017, Panama, one of the most important diplomatic allies of Taipei for 106 years, and the PRC government released a joint declaration of establishing diplomatic relations, while simultaneously "cutting off any official relations and contacts with Taiwan administration." The dominoes continued to fall when the Dominican Republic, Burkina Faso, and El Salvador followed suit to sever their diplomatic ties with Taipei in 2018.

Being one of Taiwan's long-term strongholds of diplomatic support, there were still six island states in the Pacific area that officially recognized Taipei rather than Beijing as of 2018. However, the diplomatic architecture began to teeter when it was reported that more Pacific island states were seeking to "collectively engage" with Beijing for better and stronger relations.[39] As Joseph Wu, the foreign minister of Taipei, warned on March 4, 2019, Taipei's official relations with several existing diplomatic allies are "unstable" even though it has tried its best to preserve them. On September 16, 2019, the Solomon Islands, a 36-year-long diplomatic ally of Taipei, switched recognition to PRC. Just four days later, Kiribati, another Pacific island country, cut off its official ties with Taipei and opened diplomatic and commercial connections with Beijing on September 20. On December 9, 2021, just as President Biden invited two Taiwanese officials to join the virtual "Summit for Democracy," Nicaragua officially broke diplomatic relations with Taipei and recognized in a statement that "there is only one China in the world."[40] By the end of 2021, Taipei's remaining allies were reduced from 22 to 14, including 13 nations and the Vatican, since Tsai took office.

With the expansion of Beijing's economic and diplomatic influence across the globe, it is no surprise to see more states still recognizing Taipei shifting their diplomatic positions in the near future. Earlier in 2021, there were already some sources talking about the possible "shift in position" of Honduras and the Vatican on Taiwan. In September 2021, Taipei was alarmed again by the likelihood of a diplomatic flip of Honduras, which has had formal relations with Taipei for 80 years, after the election of a pro-Beijing candidate.[41] As for a unique religious entity like the Vatican, despite pressure from the US, it has increasingly developed bilateral relations with China since the historic agreement on the appointment of Roman Catholic bishops, which was signed in 2018 and later extended in 2020. Analysts have commented that "the Holy See is taking a wait-and-see approach to cutting ties with Taipei and connecting with Beijing."[42]

The second frontier is the participation of the Taiwan administration in various international organizations, especially intergovernmental organizations. Under the administration of President Ma, Taipei had been invited, with the assistance and permission from Beijing, to participate in the World Health Assembly (WHA) meeting with observer status from 2009 to 2016, and the International Civil Aviation Organization (ICAO) meeting as a "guest" in 2013. On the heel of the degradation of the cross-Strait relations, after the DPP refused to accept the one-China principle, Beijing blocked the WHO from issuing invitations for Taipei to participate in its assembly meetings from 2017 to 2021. Given Beijing's resolute opposition, Taipei was also excluded from a series of international assemblies, including the April 2016 World Steel Conference in Brussels, Belgium; the November 2016 assembly meeting of the United Nations Framework Convention on Climate Change in Paris, France; and the May 2017 International Kimberley Process annual meeting in Perth, Australia.[43] In 2016 and 2019, even though supported by the US and some European countries, Taipei was not been invited to take part in the ICAO assembly held in Montreal, Canada. Taipei lodged a protest when the Denmark-headquartered Global Wind Organization (GWO), a non-profit organization established by globally leading wind turbine manufacturers and owners, changed to identify Taipei as "Taiwan, province of China" in May 2019. However, Taipei's protest was declined by the GWO, which responded that such a change was based on the requirement of the United Nations and the International Standards Organization (ISO).[44] Because of Beijing's strong opposition, Taipei's application for participation in the International Criminal Police Organization (Interpol) General Assembly in 2019 expectedly ended in failure.[45]

In September 2020, Taipei's Tourism Bureau tried to use the name "Taiwan Tourism Bureau" to register for the Pacific Asia Travel Association's (PATA) Travel Mart, which opened on September 23 in Sichuan Province of mainland China, instead of under the previous title "PATA Chinese Taipei Chapter." However, on September 9, the bureau discovered that its title had been changed to "Taiwan Strait Tourist Association" by the PATA. After lodging several protests against the name change, the bureau declared to withdraw from the event.[46] It is clear that Taipei's international participation after the DPP took the office has been visibly diminished due to Beijing's steadfast opposition and intervention.[47]

The third frontier is the name rectification of Taiwan's foreign offices and institutes. To countries with official relations with the PRC, Beijing asked them to prevent Taipei from illegally or improperly using the terms "Republic of China (ROC)" or "Taiwan" in their unofficial office names, in order to prevent Taipei from being misinterpreted as an independent state or government alike the PRC. In January 2017, Taipei's quasi-embassy, titled "Business Delegation of the ROC in the Federal Republic of Nigeria," was required by the Nigerian government to rename itself as "Trade Representative Office of Taipei in Lagos," as well as to move out of Abuja, the capital of Nigeria, to Lagos city, the economic center of the country. Subsequently, some other foreign offices of the Taiwanese administration with "ROC" or "Taiwan" in their names, such as those in Jordan, Bahrain, Ecuador, the United Arab Emirates, Papua New Guinea, and Fiji, were required by host governments to change their names to "Trade Representative Office of Taipei" in accordance with the one-China principle.[48] Meanwhile, the name-rectification competition also extended into the business circle. For example, in April 2018, 44 foreign airline companies were instructed by the Chinese Civil Aviation Administration to stop using "Taiwan" or "Taiwan ROC" when they refer to Taiwan on their official websites. Before July 25, 2018, the deadline set by Beijing, most of the airlines complied with this rectification requirement and adjusted in different ways to avoid using any nomenclature that would implicitly suggest an acknowl-edgement of Taiwanese sovereignty.[49]

According to an agreement reached between the Taiwan administra-tion and the Republic of Guyana in January 2021, Taipei announced set-ting up a "Taiwan Office" on February 4 and hailed it as a "diplomatic breakthrough." However, under pressure from Beijing, just one day after Taipei's announcement, Guyana terminated the agreement on February 5 and reaffirmed its adherence to the one-China principle.[50] In October 2021, Taipei announced it would set up a representative office in Lithuania's capi-tal city of Vilnius, the first such office in Europe to have "Taiwan" in the name, instead of Taipei. Furious, Beijing immediately voiced opposition and blamed it as an "attempt to create 'two Chinas' or 'one China, one Taiwan' in the world."[51] Facing insistence by Lithuania on allowing Taipei to open a "representative office" under the name of "Taiwan" in disregard of Beijing's repeated articulation of potential consequences, Beijing halted freight trains to Lithuania, stopped issuing food export permits, and recalled its ambassador to Lithuania and demanded the Lithuanian government recall its ambassador to China on October 8, 2021. After the Taiwan office, a de facto embassy, was formally opened in Lithuania, Beijing officially downgraded its diplomatic ties with Lithuania to the "charge d'affaires" level on November 21, 2021.

Track of engagement in low-political areas

Despite the confrontational approaches adopted in security, political, and diplomatic areas after Tsai took office, Beijing has, to a large extent, cho-sen to continue its engaging and accommodative policy in economic, cul-tural, and social areas. During the Ma administration, economic, cultural, and social exchanges between the Mainland and Taiwan witnessed boom-ing growth right after the implementation of the Three Links in 2008 and strengthened by more than a dozen agreements to regulate and facilitate the ever-growing interactions. Even though it is discontent with Tsai's mainland policy, Beijing still believes that economic cooperation and civil exchanges are the irreplaceable mediator and damper for the turbulent cross-Strait relations.[52] Compared with the close business, cultural, and personal links under Ma's administration, there is no doubt that the two-way economic and social exchanges have somewhat cooled since 2016, especially involving the mainland investment and tourists to Taiwan, because of the increasing tension across the Strait. However, Beijing has neither suspended or abol-ished any cross-Strait agreements ranging from economic coordination to judiciary cooperation to investment protection, nor completely cut off civil communication and local exchanges.[53]

Although inflamed by the DPP's repudiation of the one-China principle, Beijing decided to widen and deepen "integrated development" (*ronghe fazhan*) across the Strait mainly through a unilateral approach, instead of expecting mutual efforts and reciprocal measures from Taipei. In the report to the 19th National Congress of the CPC delivered by President Xi in October 2017, Beijing proclaimed to further "expand cross-Strait economic and cultural exchanges and cooperation for mutual benefits," with a prominent emphasis on ensuring people from Taiwan "enjoy the same treatment as local people when they pursue their education, start businesses, seek jobs, or settle on the mainland."[54] In his January 2, 2019, speech, Xi reiterated that the mainland will "treat Taiwan compatriots equally," and ensure people and enterprises from Taiwan "receive the same treatment as those from the mainland."[55] On March 15, 2019, Premier Li Keqiang announced again that Beijing intends to introduce more preferential policies toward Taiwanese to attract them to come to the mainland.[56] Li reemphasized on March 11, 2021, that Beijing will continue to allow Taiwanese to share the development opportunities of the mainland and continue to "promote cross-strait integration and development."[57]

In accordance with the aforementioned guiding doctrine, the mainland unveiled 31 preferential measures on February 28, 2018, covering the fields of industry, finance and taxation, land use, employment, education, and health care. The essential objective of Beijing is to integrate Taiwan more closely with the mainland economically and socially by granting Taiwanese and their companies more "national treatments" for career development as their mainland counterparts, including investing in state-owned enterprises, taking part in the Belt and Road Initiative and the Made in China 2025 project, initiating innovative start-ups, easier access to mainland cultural industries, less restrictions on film-making investment, and better protection of Taiwanese patents.[58] Since the introduction of the 31 preferential measures, it was reported that more than 2,000 enterprises with investment from Taiwan had enjoyed preferential tax treatment on the mainland and more than 100 enterprises had secured special financial support under programs for industrial transformation and upgrading, green manufacturing, and intelligent manufacturing.[59]

Additionally, Beijing annulled administrative restrictions on high-skilled professionals and technical personnel from 134 listed professions in order to attract as many well-educated Taiwanese as possible to open businesses and lead a life on the mainland. Since September 1, 2018, Taiwan residents who have lived in mainland China for six months or more with a stable job and accommodations were eligible to apply for a residence permit. Upon granting of the residence permit, permit holders can enjoy better public services and be given access to three basic rights, six services, and nine further facilitation measures, including social insurance, employment, education, and medical care.[60] Given that there are currently as many as one million Taiwanese living in the mainland, many of whom are operating Taiwanese factories, an amended regulation for individual income tax law was introduced in December 2018.[61] Shortly afterward, an amendment intending to provide preferential treatment to Taiwanese who have lived on the mainland with an extended exemption period took effect on January 1, 2019.

Following the central government's policies, 24 provinces and 72 cities on the mainland subsequently introduced hundreds of measures for implementation by the end of February 2019.[62] For instance, as one of the key pivots for cross-Strait economic and trade exchanges where more than 12,488 Taiwan-funded enterprises have been established by 2018, Shanghai launched 55 local favorable policies in June 2018. These measures allow Taiwanese law professionals to participate in the mediation of commercial cases involving Taiwanese entrepreneurs in Shanghai, permit the city's arbitration institutions to hire Taiwanese professionals, and encourage Taiwan-funded enterprises to take part in Shanghai's key development projects.

Another example of Beijing's determination and sincerity was the introduction of the 36 measures unveiled by the Supreme People's Court of mainland China on March 27, 2019, just two months after President Xi underscored the goal of strengthening cross-Strait economic integration in his January 2 speech. The 36 measures intended to provide judicial service for Taiwanese by addressing the judicial difficulty of the implementation of the 31 preferential measures, among which "twelve of them are for fully ensuring litigation rights of Taiwan compatriots, with nine providing them with quality judicial service, seven for further enhancing safeguard mechanism and eight for promoting cross-Straits judicial exchange."[63] Beijing added 26 measures on November 4, 2019, a new pack of policies for promoting cross-Strait economic and cultural exchanges and cooperation that was unveiled by the State Council Taiwan Affairs Office and the National Development and Reform Commission of the mainland. Even though it was immediately rebuked and discredited by Tsai's administration as a "ploy" to lure and divide Taiwan, this new package of policies has gained plaudits from Taiwanese enterprises because they are now subject to equal treatment as their mainland counterparts when issuing bonds to raise capital on the mainland and investing in projects such as 5G technology, civil aviation, airport construction, and theme parks. Taiwanese citizens are also entitled to seek consular protection as Chinese citizens while abroad.[64]

In the wake of the outbreak of the COVID-19 pandemic, Beijing introduced 11 preferential measures on May 15, 2020, to help Taiwan-funded enterprises on the mainland resume work and production, coordinate and promote major projects involving Taiwan-funded firms, and encourage

Taiwan-funded enterprises to participate in infrastructure construction programs. Shortly afterward, Jiangsu, Guangdong, Zhejiang, and Yunnan Provinces successively proposed special supportive measures to pandemic-stricken Taiwanese companies to address intractable problems ranging from logistics to supply chain to capital turnover.[65] On March 17, 2021, Beijing put forward a new bunch of favorable measures, known as "22 measures on agriculture and forestry," and a new guiding framework of policies to support the development of Taiwan-funded firms involved in agriculture and forestry on the mainland.[66] Those measures cover a variety of aspects including the use of agricultural and forest land, investment and business operation, research and development, local market exploration, construction and upgrade of agricultural zones, and financing and funding assistance.[67]

It is evident that Beijing has displayed an unyielding interest in strengthening, rather than weakening, the continuous dynamism of cross-Strait economic and trade exchanges. For instance, the Economic Cooperation Framework Agreement (ECFA), a trade pact which came into force on September 12, 2010, during Ma's administration and which has been denounced by Tsai and other DPP politicians as a threat undermining Taiwan's economy, has become the basis of economic collaboration between the two sides, particularly benefiting Taiwan's economic development and exportation to the mainland. Given the deterioration of cross-Strait relations since Tsai took office, it was speculated that the agreement could be terminated as the ten-year period of validity would expire in 2020. However, despite the rumors, Beijing stated explicitly in September 2020 that the agreement would be smoothly implemented as long as cross-Strait relations develop peacefully. Unsurprisingly, the MAC of Taiwan welcomed the decision and confirmed to the Taiwanese that all signed cross-Strait agreements, including the preferential ECFA, remained effective. These policies are a great lifeline to the Taiwanese economy, which was suffering during the COVID-19 pandemic.[68]

Beijing's accommodative efforts achieved effective results despite the political deadlock. After a temporary slide in 2016, the cross-Strait trade quickly resumed upward momentum in 2017.[69] The trade volume rose to US$199.4 billion, up 11.3% from 2016. Mainland exports to Taiwan totaled US$44 billion, a 9.3% increase, and imports from Taiwan stood at US$155.4 billion, up 11.9%. Taiwan's trade surplus increased 15.4% from 2016. In 2018, the cross-Strait trade volume set a historical record and totaled US$226.3 billion, an increase of 13.2% over 2017. Mainland exports to Taiwan totaled US$48.7 billion, a 10.6% increase, and imports from Taiwan stood at US$177.6 billion, up 13.9%. Taiwan's trade surplus with the mainland amounted from US$111.5 billion in 2017 to US$128.9 billion, an increase of 15.6% from 2017.[70]

Despite being affected by the COVID-19 pandemic outbreak in January 2020, Taiwan's exports to the mainland and Hong Kong totaled US$200.7 billion in 2020, a 16% increase over that of 2019. Simultaneously, Taiwan's imports from the mainland and Hong Kong increased by 9.1% to US$60.1 billion, both the highest ever. According to Taipei's finance authority, Taiwan's exports to the mainland and Hong Kong accounted for 43.9% of Taiwan's total exports in 2020, a 12% increase from 2019 and the record high in the past ten years in terms of Taiwan's export dependence on the mainland market.[71] The booming cross-Strait trade contributed to Taiwan's remarkable economic performance in 2020, 2.98% GDP growth compared to the global average of −4.5%, and outgrew the mainland's for the first time in three decades, when most countries globally plunged into recession because of the pandemic.[72] In 2021, the momentum of cross-Strait economic and trade exchanges was maintained. The latest figures released by mainland customs authorities in January 2022, indicated that cross-Strait trade soared 26% from 2020 to US$328.3 billion. The mainland's exports to Taiwan amounted to US$78.4 billion, up 30.4%, while the mainland's imports from Taiwan jumped 24.7% to US$249.9 billion.Taiwan's trade surplus with the mainland grew by US$31.1 billion from US$140.5 billion in 2020 to US$171.5 billion in 2021, also a new record high figure (Figure 3.1 and Table 3.1).[73]

In 2016, Taiwan was the mainland's seventh largest trade partner and sixth biggest source of imports. In 2018, Taiwan rose to the fifth largest trade partner and the third biggest source of imports of the mainland. In 2020, Taiwan fell down to the eighth trade partner but was still the third biggest source of imports of the mainland. On the other hand, mainland China has remained the biggest trade partner, largest export market, and source of a surplus of Taiwan ever since 2008. The economic interdependence between the two sides has further deepened instead of weakening, even though Tsai's administration vowed to keep the mainland at arm's length.[74]

In terms of investments, the mainland approved 3,517 Taiwan-invested projects in 2016, with the actual use of Taiwanese capital reaching US$1.96 billion, up 27.7% from the previous year.[75] In 2017, 3,464 Taiwan-invested projects had been approved and US$1.77 billion Taiwanese capital was actually used, with a drop of 1.5% and 9.7%, respectively, because of the stricter scrutiny of the Tsai administration.[76] Even though buoyed by the mainland's preferential policies and measures, a total of 4,911 projects had been approved in 2018 – which is up a dramatic 41.8% – nonetheless, the actual use of capital from Taiwan reduced to US$1.39 billion, down 21.5%. However, the actual use of Taiwan funds by the mainland in 2018 reached US$5.03 billion, an annual increase of 6.4%.[77] In 2019, 5,252 projects and US$1.59 billion investment were approved, up 6.9% and

14.1%, respectively, from 2018. Affected by the lingering COVID-19 pandemic and stricter regulation imposed upon mainland-oriented investment by Taipei, the actual use of capital in 2020 reached just US$1 billion, a decrease of 37.3%; while the number of the approved projects dropped to 5,105, down 2.8% slightly in comparison with 2019.[78] Nonetheless, in the first seven months of 2021, the mainland approved 3,552 Taiwan investment projects, up 47% from a year ago. Investments by Taiwanese enterprises totaled US$640 million in the first seven months, up 9.6% from the same period last year.[79] Despite the fluctuation of the capital flow from Taiwan to the mainland, the investment from Taiwanese enterprises has not been substantially strangled by the aggravating cross-Strait relations (Figure 3.2 and Table 3.2).

Instead, Beijing has always tried to encourage Taiwanese companies to invest on the mainland and helped them to achieve industrial upgrade by providing preferential policies and reducing production costs and taxation burdens.[80] In March 2017, the world-leading chipmaker, Taiwan Semiconductor Manufacturing Company (TSMC), invested US$3 billion in Nanjing to establish a subsidiary managing a 12-inch wafer fab and a design service center, despite severe opposition and repeated warnings from the

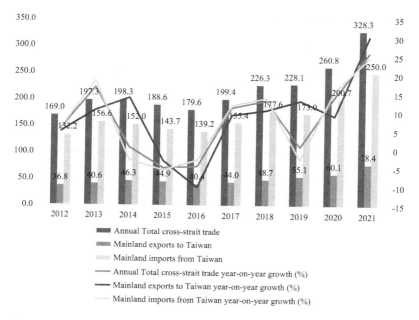

Figure 3.1 Cross-Strait trade (2012–2021) (per US$ billion).

Table 3.1 Cross-Strait trade (2012–2021) (per US$ billion)

Year	Annual total cross-Strait trade	Year-on-year growth (%)	Mainland exports to Taiwan	Year-on-year growth (%)	Mainland imports from Taiwan	Year-on-year growth (%)
2012	169.0	5.6	36.8	4.8	132.2	5.8
2013	197.3	16.7	40.6	10.5	156.6	18.5
2014	198.3	0.6	46.3	13.9	152.0	–2.8
2015	188.6	–4.9	44.9	–3	143.7	–5.5
2016	179.6	–4.5	40.4	–10.1	139.2	–2.8
2017	199.4	11.3	44.0	9.3	155.4	11.9
2018	226.3	13.2	48.7	10.6	177.6	13.9
2019	228.1	0.8	55.1	13.2	173.0	–2.6
2020	260.8	14.3	60.1	9.1	200.7	16
2021	328.3	26	78.4	30.4	249.9	24.7

Source: The General Administration of Customs of PRC, Cross-Strait Trade Statistics by Year, The author added the figures of 2021. http://www.gwytb.gov.cn/local/201805/t20180524_11958201.htm, access via the Taiwan Affairs Office of the State Council of PRC.

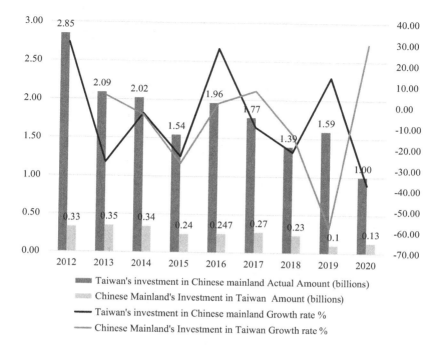

Figure 3.2 Cross-Strait investment (2012–2020) (per US$ billion).

Table 3.2 Cross-Strait investment (2012–2020) (per US$ billion)

Year	Taiwan's investment in the Chinese mainland		Chinese mainland's Investment in Taiwan	
	Actual amount (billions)	Growth rate (%)	Amount (billions)	Growth rate (%)
2012	2.85	30.4	0.33	—
2013	2.09	−26.7	0.35	5.12
2014	2.02	−3.30	0.34	−4.01
2015	1.54	−23.80	0.24	−27.16
2016	1.96	27.7	0.247	1.64
2017	1.77	−9.70	0.27	7.69
2018	1.39	−21.50	0.23	−13.16
2019	1.59	14.1	0.1	−58.01
2020	1	−37.30	0.13	29.9

Source: Ministry of the Commerce of PRC, Taiwan, Hong Kong and Macao Department, The Statistics of Mainland-Taiwan Trade and Economic Cooperation, 2020, http://tga.mofcom.gov.cn/article/sjzl/taiwan

Note: Investment transited from the third place is not included.

Tsai administration. TSMC Chairman Morris Chang explained that with this first factory capable of producing 16 nanometer chips, it could help TSMC expand business opportunities to take advantage of the rapid growth of the mainland Chinese semiconductor market.[81] The United Microelectronics Corp., Taiwan's second-largest contract chipmaker, declared in July 2017 that it would invest US$611 million to expand its factory in Xiamen City. Two months later, the Foxconn Technology Group, the world's largest electronics contractor, reached a cooperation agreement with the Nanjing City government to invest US$5.7 billion in the production of liquid crystal displays and intelligent terminal devices and to conduct research and development in information technology. In May 2018, mainland China's securities regulator approved the application of Foxconn Industrial Internet Co., Ltd., a subsidiary of Foxconn Technology Group, for an initial public offering to issue 1.97 billion shares on the Shanghai Stock Exchange. The total investment of 27.253 billion RMB made the company a big winner in China's A-share market.[82] In the face of a harsh struggle involving semiconductor supply chain and technology between the US and China, TSMC approved a capital expenditure of US$2.89 billion on April 23, 2021, to increase the process capacity of its 28-nanometer-chip plant in Nanjing. It is planned the production line will start mass production in the second half of 2022 and double the monthly production capacity to 40,000 pieces by 2023. This plan was welcomed by Beijing with open arms.

Banking industry cooperation across the Strait has also achieved steady progress despite the political impasse. Since September 2010, a handful of private banks based in Taiwan have received approval from the China Bank Regulatory Commission to set up branches on the mainland. However, Taiwan-funded enterprises, especially small- and medium-sized companies, have been universally vexed by difficulties in financing for many years because of the inefficient banking service and lagging financial cooperation between the two sides. After Minister Zhang Zhijun promised in February 2017 to give bigger market access to Taiwan's financial institutes, two Taiwanese banks, Chang Hwa Commercial Bank and Cathay United Bank, won approval to upgrade their branches in Nanjing and Shanghai to subsidiaries with independent entity quality in July. One year later, the Cathay United Bank celebrated the opening of its Shanghai subsidiary in September 2018, the first of Taiwanese banks on the mainland, to specifically address the financing issues of Taiwanese companies. On November 30, 2018, Taiwan Fubon Financial Holding Co. completed the transfer of 19.95% shares of Xiamen Bank held by its wholly owned subsidiary Fubon Bank (Hong Kong) and thereupon became the second-largest shareholder of Xiamen Bank in December 1, a new breakthrough in cross-Strait financial cooperation. In comparison with the previous model of indirect shareholding through a third-place subsidiary, it was the first time that a Taiwanese financial institution was approved to directly invest in a mainland bank, reflecting the deepening of cross-Strait financial exchanges and cooperation.[83]

According to the information released by the TAO in September 2021, there are already 42 A-shares–listed Taiwan enterprises, after 4 more companies were newly listed on the mainland stock market in 2021with more waiting for approval. Some Taiwan-funded financial institutions, including Taipei Fubon Bank and Bank of Taiwan Securities Investment Trust, are encouraged to apply for the Qualified Foreign Institutional Investor Qualification in order to invest in the mainland securities market.[84] The statistics provided by the Financial Supervisory Commission of the Taiwanese administration indicated that cross-Strait cooperation in the financial sector has continuously improved. As of the end of August 2021, four securities investment trust enterprises (SITEs) have received approval in the mainland and are already in operation there. In addition, six Taiwanese securities companies have established eight representative offices in the mainland, and one securities investment trust company has opened a representative office. Twenty-one Taiwanese SITEs and two securities companies have received recognition as qualified foreign institutional investors (QFIIs) from the mainland securities regulatory authority. Ten Taiwanese insurers have applied for recognition as QFIIs, been recognized by the mainland securities regulatory authority, and approved to invest up to a maximum of $US4.7 billion. In addition, eight Taiwanese insurers have established eight representative offices in the mainland.[85]

In comparison with the consistency of encouraging cross-Strait economic, trade, and financial cooperation after the inauguration of Tsai in May 2016, Beijing's change of policies toward Taiwanese tourism has led to a steady reduction of personnel exchanges. Discouraged by the deterioration of cross-Strait relations, the number of mainland tourists to Taiwan plummeted from 4.36 million in 2015, a historical record, to 3.64 million in 2016, a drop-off of 16.3%. In 2017, the number slumped to 2.9 million and reached the lowest point since 2012. However, in contrast with the decreasing mainland visitors to Taiwan, personnel exchanges across the Strait have not dwindled because of the steady swelling of Taiwanese visitors to the mainland. For example, in 2018, more than 9 million people traveled across the Strait. The mainland received 6.1 million Taiwanese visitors, including 0.4 million Taiwanese who paid their first visit to the mainland, with both being record highs.[86] With the escalation of cross-Strait tension, on August 1, 2019, Beijing suspended a program allowing individual tourists from 47 mainland cities to visit Taiwan. The suspension of this program, launched in 2011, brought forth a sharp decline of individual mainland Chinese tourists, even though business travelers and organized tour groups are still allowed to visit Taiwan (Figure 3.3 and Table 3.3).

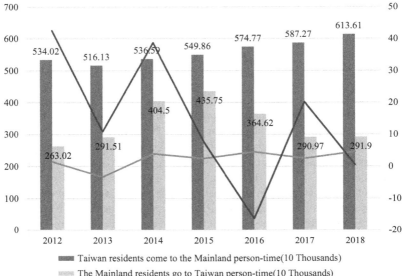

Figure 3.3 Cross-Strait personnel exchanges (2012–2018). (Note: Numbers represent 10,000 people.)

Table 3.3 Cross-Strait personnel exchanges (2012–2018)

Year	Taiwan residents coming to the mainland		Mainland residents going to Taiwan	
	Persons (ten thousands)	Growth rate (%)	Persons (ten thousands)	Growth rate (%)
2012	534.02	1.47	263.02	42.56
2013	516.13	−3.31	291.51	10.86
2014	536.59	3.96	404.5	38.76
2015	549.86	2.47	435.75	7.72
2016	574.77	4.53	364.62	−16.3
2017	587.27	2.49	290.97	20.2
2018	613.61	4.58	291.9	0.51

Source: Sun Yafu, *40 Years of Cross-Straits Relations (1979–2019)* (Beijing: Jiuzhou Press, 2020), 323.

Meanwhile, in the name of "resisting mainland China's interference," Taipei successfully finished the amendments to the Criminal Law, National Secret Protection Law, National Security Law, and Act Governing Relations Between the People of the Taiwan Area and the Mainland Area in 2019. In the same vein, on December 31, 2019, the DPP-controlled Legislative Yuan passed the Anti-Infiltration Act, which took effect on January 15, 2020. This law authorized Taiwan authorities to censor Taiwanese with mainland connections to prevent "external hostile intervention" in Taiwan's political processes.[87] Through these measures, Tsai's administration has established an oversight mechanism for cross-Strait personnel exchanges. Along with the spread of the COVID-19 pandemic, Taipei declared on February 7, 2020, that it would shut off passenger transportation between Xiamen City in the mainland and Kinmen County in Taiwan, known as the "mini three links." A day later, Taipei expanded the restriction to the "big three links" by suspending most of the direct passenger ship routes and air lines across the Taiwan Strait.[88] From then on, the door of cross-Strait personnel exchanges has been largely closed by the ongoing pandemic and escalating tension between the two sides.

Track of suppression against pro-independence figures

Civil and local exchanges and cooperation have been regarded by Beijing as an indispensable way to enhance cross-Strait mutual understanding and trust. During the Ma administration, Beijing had neither prohibited pro-independence politicians and local leaders from conducting high-profile cross-Strait interactions nor imposed visible restrictions on pro-DPP businesspeople and public figures seeking to do business on the mainland. After the DPP returned to power, Beijing has relentlessly closed the door for any communication with DPP leaders and extended a strategy of "precision strikes" to target those who publicly express pro-DPP or pro-independence views.

First, Beijing has moved to disengage from green camp politicians. Since Ma took office, Beijing has actively conducted dialogues and kept lines of communication with some of the leading figures of the DPP and local governments under DPP's rule, without persisting in demanding they publicly endorse the one-China principle, in order to encourage DPP politicians to pragmatically adjust their pro-independence stance through in-depth interaction. For instance, Chen Chu, the mayor of Kaohsiung City and a prominent founder of the DPP, paid a visit to Beijing in May 2009 to promote the 2009 World Games in her hometown, the birthplace and a longstanding stronghold of the DPP. During this trip, which made her the highest-ranking member of the DPP to travel to the mainland while in office, she was received by the mayor of Beijing, as well Minister Zhang Zhijun of the TAO. Her visit was also appraised as an ice-breaking event for the party-to-party exchanges between the CPC and the DPP. At the invitation of Chen Chu, 148 mainland athletes joined the Kaohsiung World Games, the first international comprehensive sports meet held by Taiwan.

In October 2012, the ex-DPP chairman and ex-Premier of the Executive Yuan, Hsieh Chang-ting, was invited to visit the mainland and received by Minister Wang Yi, the then director of the TAO, aiming to "hear the rational, positive and constructive opinions and advices about the cross-Strait relations" from DPP leading figures.[89] Mayor Chen started her second trip to the mainland on August 9, 2013, to invite counterpart mainland mayors to attend the Asia-Pacific Cities Summit hosted in Kaohsiung in September. As a gesture of goodwill, five cities on the mainland, including Tianjin, Shenzhen, and Xiamen, sent mayoral-level delegations to take part in the summit.[90] In June 2014, Lai Ching-te, the mayor of Tainan City and known for his outspoken pro-independence position, was invited to make his first visit to mainland China and attend the opening ceremony of an art exhibition in Shanghai. The mayor of Taoyuan City, Zheng Wen-can, a rising star of the DPP, set up the Taoyuan–Hong Kong Exchange Forum when he visited Hong Kong in May 2015 after he assumed office in December 2014.

However, after the DPP resumed the presidency in 2016, Beijing began to place much stricter constraints on communication with DPP politicians based on the explicit recognition of the one-China principle. From then on, all the official interactions between the mainland and Taiwan's DPP administration, ranging from central to local governmental level, were stalled. Take Kaohsiung City as an example, even though Mayor Chen Chu tried to copy the successful Asia-Pacific Cities Summit model and extended invitations to several mainland mayors to participate in the Global Harbor Cities Forum held in September 2016, no mainland city responded to her invitation. Similarly, the aforementioned Taoyuan–Hong Kong Exchange Forum was suspended, and city-to-city cooperation in tourism, airline transportation, the logistics industry, and the convention and exhibition industry was blocked. In October 2014, with assistance from Beijing, the East Asian Olympic Committee (EAOC) granted Taichung City the right to host the 2019 East Asian Youth Games, the first international multisport event for countries in East Asia organized by the EAOC. One month later, Lin Chia-lung, a deep-green heavyweight of the DPP, won the position of mayor of Taichung in the "nine-in-one" local election. However, Beijing had not taken any opposing actions, even though it was disappointed by the party shift of the city, until some Taiwanese groups in February 2018 started to push forward a referendum on using the "proper name," implying possible use of "Republic of China" or "Taiwan" rather than "Chinese

Taipei," to participate in future international sports events, including the 2020 Tokyo Olympics. Such a referendum proposal, allowed by the Tsai administration, was deemed by Beijing as a "flagrant challenge" to the Olympic model, as well as a provocative denial of the one-China principle. Given that some political forces continued to push forward the referendum after the International Olympic Committee reaffirmed that there was no chance to reconsider any change to the name of the Chinese Taipei Olympic Committee, at an emergency meeting of the EAOC convened by Beijing in July 2018, the EAOC decided to revoke the hosting right of Taichung City for the 2019 East Asian Youth Games.[91]

With the significant deterioration of cross-Strait relations during Tsai's second term, Beijing strengthened its pressure upon the DPP camp, especially on radical pro-independence advocates on the island. It was reported by Hong Kong media that in November 2020, Beijing started to develop a "list of Taiwan secessionists activists," accusing them of the offense of splitting the state according to the Anti-Secession Law and National Security Law. On May 12, 2021, for the first time, the TAO singled out Joseph Wu as a "Taiwan independence die-hard" and vowed to "take any necessary punitive measures."[92] Liu Junchuan, the deputy minister of the TAO, warned on October 29, 2021, that Beijing would mete out punishment to the "Taiwan independence die-hards in accordance with the law" and "hold the secessionist accountable for life."[93]

On November 5, 2021, the TAO unprecedentedly declared concrete measures on laws to punish "die-hard secessionists," including prohibiting them and their families from entering the mainland and the Hong Kong and Macao special administrative regions, and restricting their associated institutions from cooperating with organizations and individuals in the mainland. By specifically calling out three prominent DPP politicians – Soo Tsing-tshiong, the leader of Taiwan's Executive Yuan; You Si-kun, the head of Taiwan's Legislative Yuan; and Joseph Wu, foreign minister of Tsai's administration – Beijing accused them of "colluding with foreign forces to split China" and "actively pushing the de facto independence" of the island and pledged to "seek criminal responsibility for them, valid for life."[94] This is the first time Beijing moved to slap sanctions against Taiwan secessionists, marking a significant move from repeated verbal warnings to concrete punitive actions.

Second, Beijing also moved to boycott "pro-independence entertainers." In the past several decades, the cultural and artistic exchanges and cooperation across the Strait have increased rapidly. Numerous Taiwanese artists came to the mainland for career development given the large and growing market. However, with the deterioration of cross-Strait relations, the pro-independence stance of some Taiwan entertainment industry figures, including singers, writers, actors, and directors, has repeatedly led to backlash for themselves and their works. As early as July 2016, a famous Taiwanese actor, Leon Dai, was fired from a film titled *No Other Love* in which he played a leading role even though the shoot had already been completed in June. The major critique of him was his "ambiguous stance over the country and national identity," showcased by his support to the Sunflower Movement, a one-month protest that occurred in 2014 in Taiwan against the Cross-Strait Service Trade Agreement and closer relations between Taiwan and the mainland.[95]

Similarly, the mainland "netizens" (*wangmin*) launched a massive online campaign in January 2017 to boycott *Village of No Return*, a film directed by Taiwanese Chen Yu-Hsun, for his sympathetic attitude toward the Sunflower Movement. Right after Beijing revealed the 31 preferential measures to Taiwanese, including smoothing the way for Taiwan's movie industry to collaborate with its mainland counterpart and providing unprecedented opportunities and access for cross-Strait film and television cooperation, TAO spokesperson An Fengshan stated explicitly in March 2018 that Beijing "would not permit the release of films in China whose production include entertainers who hold pro-Taiwan independence views and propagate pro-Taiwanese independence speeches."[96] It is the first time that Beijing issued such a clear-cut warning to those so-called pro-Taiwan independence entertainers. Consequently, on March 29, 2018, the screening of the *Missing Johnny*, a Taiwanese film starring Lawrence Ko and originally scheduled for release in April, had been "indefinitely suspended" on the mainland, because of Ko's pro-Taiwan independence opinions and comments that had been exposed and disseminated on mainland China's social media.[97] Even though Beijing continues to encourage cross-Strait film and television exchanges, and welcomes Taiwanese entertainers to pursue career development on the mainland, the spokesperson of the TAO reiterated on April 30, 2021, that Beijing would not allow some Taiwanese entertainers to make money on the mainland while supporting separatist activities.

In October 2021, the Taiwanese film *Time Machine* was announced and planned to be released simultaneously in mainland China, Hong Kong, Macao, and Taiwan. However, a large number of mainland netizens soon questioned and opposed the film after they discovered the film producer had received funding from the Taiwanese administration, and that Tsai Yifen, the Taiwanese director and screenwriter of the film, had reportedly made comments supporting Taiwan and Hong Kong independence. Just a few days after the camera was turned on, the lead actor, Chen Linong, a Taiwanese artist active in the mainland, withdrew from the film. Due to the large backlash, the film production company also issued a statement on October 25, stating that Tsai Yifen has resigned as director and screenwriter.

Third, Beijing has also moved to target green businesspeople. For many decades, Beijing has laid down numerous preferential policies and special measures to facilitate Taiwan businesspeople and companies doing business on the mainland, even if Beijing knew some of them were generous donors to the DPP and steadfast supporters of the pro-independence camp. It is also not a secret that some Taiwanese openly advocate secession in Taiwan while their relatives or patrons have been operating lucrative businesses in the mainland, or that some Taiwan businesspeople accumulate huge fortunes in the mainland market while also financing their relatives or political grantees to pursue secession or anti-mainland activities on the island. However, when more and more "double-dealers" were exposed by mainland people and the media, Beijing started to adjust its decade-long "undifferentiated" policy due to massive domestic pressure. As early as December 2015, the TAO stated clearly that Beijing "will never allow a few Taiwan businessmen to make a profit on the mainland on one hand, but to support 'Taiwan-independence' separatist behaviors and undermine the cross-Strait relations on the other hand."[98] In December 2016, Minister Zhang Zhijun, then director of the TAO, reiterated Beijing's intolerance to double-dealers who take advantage of mainland's preferential policies to make money while financing secessionist activities in Taiwan.[99]

In December 2016, Hai Pa Wang, a pro-green camp business group operating a seafood restaurant chain both in Taiwan and mainland China with close ties to Tsai's family industry, was fined by the mainland local government for failing sanitation inspections. Even though Beijing insisted that it was a legal move and was not politically motivated, Hai Pa Wang, after being accused as a "Taiwan independence supporter," issued a public statement in the form of an advertisement in a Taiwanese newspaper saying it "firmly supports the idea that both sides of the Taiwan Strait belong to one China" and it "has no relationship with President Tsai Ing-wen's family other than that between 'a tenant and a landlord.'"[100] During Tsai's stay in Los Angeles in August 2018, her visit to a branch of the 85°C Bakery Café, a Taiwan-based cafe chain that has over 600 outlets on the mainland, infuriated mainland consumers as another example of a Taiwanese company that is "trying to rake in Chinese money" while supporting Taiwanese independence. Following an online appeal for a boycott of its mainland stores by mainland netizens, the company posted a statement on its Chinese-language website to affirm its "firm support for the 1992 consensus" and "the belief that the two sides of the Strait are one family."[101]

Furthermore, Beijing started to target economic sanctions against DPP's core constituencies instead of squeezing Taiwan as a whole. For instance, the DPP has enjoyed more widespread popularity than the KMT in rural constituencies for many decades. Taiwanese peasants, compared to urban residents, are well known to be much more staunch supporters of the Taiwan independence agenda. On March 1, 2021, Beijing issued a temporary ban on the importation of pineapples from Taiwan over contamination with harmful organisms. It was the first time that cross-Strait fruit imports had been halted by Beijing. On September 18, 2021, mainland China's General Administration of Customs suspended accepting customs declarations for sugar apples and wax apples from Taiwan as a result of the repeated detection of quarantine pests on imported sugar apples and wax apples shipped to the mainland. These three items had benefited from Beijing's preferential policy since 2005 and had ranked as the top three cross-Strait fruit exports from Taiwan in terms of value since Ma's administration. For instance, Taiwan exported 41,661 metric tons of pineapples to the mainland in 2020, worth US$53.49 million and accounting for 91% of the island's total pineapple exports, according to data released by the Council of Agriculture of Taiwan authority.[102] In the first six months of 2021, however, owing to the impact of the ongoing pineapple ban, the percentage of pineapple exports to mainland China reportedly plummeted to 14%, causing Taiwan's pineapple exports to shrink by approximately 30% during this period. The fruit bans, among the targeted sanctions in a long process that kicked off in 2016, not only reflect the fact that the two sides could not deal with an issue as minor as "harmful pests" without official channels but also signaled Beijing's grave displeasure with Tsai's administration and farmer voters loyal to the DPP.[103]

Fair to say, aside from occasional civil online protests and pressure campaigns, Beijing has been fairly self-restrained and has not officially carried out punitive measures against "two-faced" individuals or companies for many years. It is noted, for example, that DPP legislator Ho Chih-wei, who is a radical Taiwan-independence advocate, has for years owned a Taiwan-funded financial leasing company in the mainland through his family business Sunny Bank. Some Taiwanese TV dramas sponsored by the famous independence-minded Sanlih Entertainment Television in Taiwan have been shown in the mainland and proven fairly profitable. The Union Bank of Taiwan, the family business of the founder of the well-known anti-mainland newspaper *Liberty Times*, Lin Rong-San, is also operating in the mainland with credit card and UnionPay card services.[104] Nonetheless, frustrated by the reelection victory of Tsai in 2020 with abundant financial support from pro-green camp businesspeople who made handsome gains from the mainland market, Beijing's patience and tolerance wore thin. Zhu Fenglian, spokesperson of the TAO, told a press conference in November 2021 that Beijing will not only seek lifelong criminal responsibility for a few stubborn secessionists but also will "prohibit the companies or paymasters of these diehard secessionists from making economic profit from Chinese mainland."[105] This statement implied that Beijing will henceforth mount severe precision strikes on two-faced individuals and companies, and cut off the capital chain between green-camp businesspeople in the mainland and pro-independence politicians in Taiwan.

Shortly after the announcement of the TAO, law enforcement agencies in five provinces and cities – Shanghai, Jiangsu, Jiangxi, Hubei, and Sichuan – reportedly carried out an inspection and investigation into Taiwan's Far East Group, a best-known generous donor to DPP politicians, including Premier Soo Tsing-tshiong and his daughter Su Qiaohui, an incumbent DPP legislator.[106] The chemical fiber textile and cement enterprises invested by the group were accused of a series of illegal and noncompliant behaviors concerning environmental protection, land use, employee occupational health, production safety, fire protection, taxation, product quality, etc. The enterprises involved thereafter had been taxed and fined 474 million RMB, equivalent to US$74.2 million. The idle construction land of the enterprise had also been recovered in accordance with relevant laws and regulations.[107] Commenting on the event, the TAO reaffirmed that Taiwan businesspeople in the mainland must draw a line in the sand and distance themselves from the secessionists.

Track of accommodation to non-green camp forces

For many years, Beijing has reiterated that "no political party, group or individual in Taiwan will have any difficulty in conducting exchanges with the mainland," provided they recognize the 1992 Consensus and that "the two sides both belong to one China."[108] On the basis of adhering to the one-China principle, Beijing started to promote party-to-party contacts with the then opposition parties of the pan-blue camp in Taiwan, including the KMT, People First Party, and New Party, amid the cross-Strait turbulence during the Chen Shuibian administration. Beijing's endeavor culminated in the meeting between President Hu Jintao and then KMT chairman Lien Chan in April 2005 in defiance of the opposition of the Chen administration.

After the DPP clutched the reins of central power in 2016, Beijing, on one hand, continued regular dialogue with the pan-blue camp via the existing "second rail" mechanism, such as the Strait Forum, to maintain mutual trust and political consensus. On the other hand, in contrast with the closed-door policy on multilayered exchanges with green camp politicians, Beijing turned to strengthen its active engagement with the local mayoral and county governments under the reign of the KMT. In September 2016, a delegation comprised of eight magistrates and mayors mainly from KMT-ruled cities and counties recognizing the 1992 Consensus was invited to visit Beijing, aiming to explore opportunities for exchanges and cooperation in the areas of economy, culture, and tourism.[109] Beijing is also actively advocating the "four links" (*sitong*) – the construction of sea-crossing bridges, as well supplies of water, electricity, and gas – from coastal areas in Fujian province to Kinmen and Matsu, two long-term strongholds of the KMT in Taiwan. In August 2018, Kinmen Island, haunted by water shortages for decades, opened a pipeline to receive fresh water supply from Jinjiang City, Fujian Province. Matsu, with an even worse freshwater supply and reserve problem, is also looking forward to following this initiative and connecting to the mainland water supply system. Additionally, both Kinmen and Matsu are trying to connect with the mainland electricity and gas grid, a project endorsed and coordinated by the Fujian provincial government, to support its growing population and local economy.[110]

In January 2019, after winning 15 out of 22 mayoral or magistrate positions in the local elections held in December 2018, the KMT established the Center for Cross-Strait Cities Exchanges aiming to promote local cooperation. Presently, Beijing has sent invitations and welcomed the leaders of those KMT-governed counties and cities to visit the mainland. The leaders of the Taichung City and Nantou County, where KMT regained power after the election, visited the mainland successively in March 2019 to expand local agricultural product exportation to the mainland by signing favorable orders and opening "green channels" for product transportation and sale.

From March 22 to 28, 2019, the newly elected KMT Kaohsiung mayor, Han Kuo-yu, who unequivocally expressed his endorsement of the 1992 Consensus during his campaign, set foot on Hong Kong, Macao, and the Chinese mainland. During his meeting with Minister Liu Jieyi of the TAO in Shenzhen City, Guangdong Province, he reasserted that the 1992 Consensus was the "anchor of cross-Strait relations" and the mainland is the key to Taiwan's prosperity and people's well-being. In response, Minister Liu stated that the mainland will continue to share development opportunities with Taiwan's residents and increase people's "sense of gain" on the basis of adhering to the one-China principle.[111] In his weeklong visit, Mayor Han signed trade deals worth more than NT$5.2 billion (about US$170 million) and agreed to launch the Kaohsiung–Shenzhen Twin-City Forum and Kaohsiung–Xiamen Twin-Harbor Forum as new institutional mechanisms to enhance trade, tourism, education, and cultural exchanges between the two sides. New direct flight and cruise routes between Kaohsiung and mainland cities aiming to bring more tourists to visit Kaohsiung were negotiated before Han declared to campaign for the presidency in 2020.

In addition to Beijing's close engagement with the local blue camp governments and figures, a new and prominent characteristic of its accommodative policy toward non-green camp political forces is Beijing's more encompassing and flexible outreach to apolitical, or politically non-independence leaning, groups in Taiwan. In 2014, Ko Wen-je, a surgeon who had no political experience, campaigned and captured a landslide victory in Taipei's mayoral race as an independent. Ko's victory was observed as the symbol of the rise of the "middle force" representing the people who are tired of the fierce partisan struggle between the green and blue camps in Taiwan's political arena.[112] By the time Ko won the mayorship, Beijing was very vigilant against his pro-DPP stance and rhetoric, such as the proposal for a "two countries, one system" formula, and the opinion that the 1992 Consensus is "a consensus without consensus."[113] Despite his ideological inclination, Ko's non-partisan nature provided him much greater flexibility to adjust his rhetoric about cross-Strait relations. Ko's statement of "understanding and respecting the 1992 Consensus," and endorsement of Beijing's doctrine that the two sides of the Strait are "one family" and "sharing a common destiny" soon after taking office received a positive response from Beijing, even though his terminology was basically an ambiguous reference, instead of a direct concession, to the one-China principle. On the face of it, Beijing decided to extend an olive branch to Ko, a long-lasting DPP supporter who identified himself as a dark-green figure in terms of his political stance.

In August 2015, Ko was welcomed by Beijing to attend the Shanghai–Taipei Forum, the first cross-Strait city-to-city exchange platform initiated in 2010 by then Taipei mayor Hau Lung-pin from the KMT. From then on, this annual twin-city forum has been continuously held and survived the deteriorating relations as the highest official channels after the DPP returned to power in May 2016.[114] It also made Ko's positive and constructive interaction with the mainland possible. For example, when Ma was still in office, the KMT-controlled Taipei municipal government won the right to host the 2017 Universiade in 2011. In the context of the cross-Strait détente, Beijing helped Taipei to compete against the other rival bidders in order to increase Taipei's global visibility. However, by the time Taipei's Universiade opened in August 2017, when the DPP was already in the saddle and cross-Strait relations were strained, Beijing decided to cooperate with Ko, instead of launching a total boycott, in order to reward his flexible attitude about cross-Strait relations. Although the mainland's delegation of athletes "technically evaded" the opening ceremony during which Tsai Ing-wen was introduced to the spectators as "president," Beijing nonetheless displayed goodwill by sending about 200 athletes and coaches to take part in the event.[115]

One month after Ko won reelection by a thin margin in November 2018, Beijing, at Ko's pressing invitation, agreed to send an upgraded delegation led by Shanghai Executive Vice Mayor Zhou Bo to take part in the forum held in Taipei. The two cities signed 3 memorandums, in addition to the other 30 signed in the previous eight forums, to further improve the civic exchanges covering sports, film, and urban development.[116] On June

6, 2019, Ko, widely perceived as a promising challenger for the upcoming 2020 presidential election, explicitly stated that the relation between the mainland and Taiwan is neither "foreign relation," nor "state-to-state relation," and "one China is not a problem."[117] His statement thereafter paved the way for the 2019 Shanghai–Taipei Forum held in Shanghai.[118]

When the cross-Strait relations were caught in rising tension after the breakout of the COVID-19 pandemic in 2020, Ko reiterated his stance that people on both sides of the Strait are "one family" and "communication is better than a blockade, cooperation is better than confrontation, and being a family is better than being enemies."[119] Ko's pragmatic attitude distanced himself from the DPP's anti-China position and was appreciated by Beijing amid the accelerating antagonism across the Strait, resulting in the holding of the 2020 Taipei–Shanghai Forum via the internet due to the pandemic in July 2020. On December 1, 2021, the seventh Taipei–Shanghai Forum during Ko's term as Taipei mayor successfully opened and three accords concerning technological and cultural cooperation were signed.

Given the rise of the middle force in Taiwan's political spectrum going beyond the traditional blue vs. green structure, Beijing's active engagement with Ko carries particular political significance. Based on its understanding of the prospect of political transformation in Taiwan, Beijing tries to display more pragmatism and flexibility by expanding engagement with various non-traditional politicians if they do not endorse Taiwan independence, rather than focus solely on keeping ties with the KMT or the pan-blue camp as before.

Conclusion: Challenges for mainland China's dual-track policy

Beijing's insistence on the acceptance of the one-China principle combined with Taipei's repudiation of the 1992 Consensus since the DPP assumed power in 2016 have pushed cross-Strait relations into a deadlock. Beijing believes the Tsai administration, under the ambiguous discourse of maintaining the status quo, is essentially trying to push forward "incremental Taiwan independence" in a salami-slicing way and institutionalize Taiwan's de facto independence. Thus, Beijing decided to tighten the noose on Taipei to contain the pro-independence momentum, including escalating military deterrence toward Taipei, adopting a no-contact policy by cutting off all levels of political communications, isolating Taiwan from the international community by resuming competition for diplomatic allies, demanding foreign companies to erase references to Taiwan, as well as restricting Taiwan's participation in multiple international organizations. In addition,

Beijing also extended the campaign of pressuring to a much wider range than before, including disengagement with local governments under the reign of the DPP, blacklisting pro-independence entertainment industry figures, and the "precision punishment" of pro-green camp businesspeople.

Even though it was determined to make the Tsai administration pay a heavy price for refusing to endorse the 1992 Consensus, Beijing steadily maintained and strengthened its engagement policy in economic, social, and cultural fields by introducing a series of favorable measures, aiming to incorporate Taiwan deeply and closely into its economic orbit. It explains why the cross-Strait trade, as well Taiwan's investment and visitors to the mainland achieved significant progress in spite of the frigid political face-off since the DPP assumed office. At the same time, Beijing intensified its accommodative approaches to non-green camp forces in Taiwan, ranging from the pan-blue camp politicians and the white force, which has no strong partisan affiliation, in order to avoid rupturing cross-Strait relations.

Beijing's dual-track policy, which promises to share economic opportunities with Taiwan while also ratcheting up pressure upon the Tsai administration, has inevitably brought some counterproductive consequences. First, Beijing's pressure in security, political, and diplomatic areas has aroused backlash from the DPP or even stimulated deep-green camp figures to advocate more radical pro-independence initiatives. For example, Beijing's tough measures pushed Taipei to step away from its original ambiguous stance on the 1992 Consensus and turn toward embracing green camp forces so as to solidify its political base. For instance, rebutting Xi's January 2, 2019, remarks, Tsai issued strongly worded messages on the same day by announcing publicly that "I must stress that we've never accepted the 1992 Consensus," and claimed that her stance represented "the consensus of the Taiwanese."[120]

Second, Beijing's engagement effort was offset by security tension and the political impasse. There is no doubt that numerous unilateral beneficiary measures unveiled by the mainland will be conducive to economic interdependence and social integration across the Taiwan Strait. However, it would not necessarily make the prospect of reunification become more welcomed by the Taiwanese. Instead, the mainland's confrontational approaches in security, political, and diplomatic frontiers would undermine the credibility and sincerity of Beijing's conciliatory gestures in economic, social, and cultural areas. The strained cross-Strait relations will inevitably exacerbate the hostility and drive common Taiwanese to turn their backs on mainland China, which will consequently make it harder, instead of easier, to charm the public into favoring Beijing's ultimate goal of peacefully unifying the two sides.

Third, Beijing's hardline stance undermines its efforts to engage with the Taiwanese public. For many decades, Beijing has endeavored to achieve reunification by "winning the hearts and minds of the Taiwan compatriots," exemplified by President Xi's reemphasis of the importance to reach "agreements in heart and soul" with Taiwan in his report to the 19th National Congress of the CPC.[121] However, given a constructive relationship requires continuous and consistent forward-leaning momentum, the enduring cross-Strait standoff unfortunately has already deepened civilian distrust and antagonism between the two societies. There are many evident signals showing that mutual suspicion, or even antipathy among ordinary people, is significantly increasing and that public opinion toward each other is rapidly deteriorating. For example, the anti-Taiwan sentiment had partly led to the plummet of tourists from the mainland to Taiwan. At the same time, Taiwan's anti-mainland emotion continues to grow, and the Chinese identity among the Taiwanese continues to decline.

However, there is little possibility for Beijing to change this dual-track policy if the DPP administration continues to reject the one-China principle. More important, it is very likely that the current "selective engagement" policy will be employed as a regular and routine framework for Beijing to deal with the Taiwanese administration if only the DPP is in power. Beijing clearly understands that the two-party political system in Taiwan means it will unavoidably have to face a DPP administration in the long run before the Taiwan issue reaches a final resolution. Unless the DPP abandons its pro-independence ideology or accepts the one-China principle, Beijing is likely to apply this kind of dual-track approach as the most feasible and effective way to cope with any DPP administration in the future. Furthermore, with the ever-expanding power asymmetry across the Taiwan Strait, Beijing will have more policy instruments in its toolbox that could enable it to adjust this fundamental framework by adopting upgraded measures.

In sum, after the DPP assumed office in 2016, the enduring political stalemate resulting from the rejection of the one-China principle is gradually transforming cross-Strait relations from "hot interaction" during the Ma administration to "cold confrontation" characterized by the combination of cooperation and conflict. The uncertainty and risks have sharply risen, making cross-Strait relations become ever-increasingly "complicated and tough" (*fuza yanjun*).[122] Currently, Beijing's pressure campaign is mainly confined in security, political, and diplomatic areas, and the tension has not yet affected the economic cooperation and social exchanges momentum, although the vibrant dynamics have definitely been somewhat eroded. Yet, the potential for the escalation of tension and head-to-head conflict across the Strait continues to slowly build.

Notes

1 Zeng Runmei, "An Analysis of Tsai Ing-wen's Proposition to 'Maintain the Status Quo' across the Taiwan Strait," *Cross-Taiwan Strait Studies*, no. 3 (2015), 39–48.
2 Scott L. Kastner, "Is the Taiwan Strait Still a Flash Point? Rethinking the Prospect for Armed Conflict between China and Taiwan," *International Security*, vol. 40, no. 3 (Winter 2015–2016), 54–92; Huang Jing, "Xi Jinping's Taiwan Policy: Boxing Taiwan in with the One-China Framework," in *Taiwan and China: Fitful Embrace*, ed. Lowell Dittmer (Oakland: University of California Press, 2017), 239–248; Chen Xiancai, "The Development of Taiwan Independence Forces after the DPP Resumed the Power," *Taiwan Studies*, no. 3 (2017), 13–22.
3 Jean-Pierre Cabestan, "Beijing's Policy towards President Tsai Ing-wen and the Future of Cross-Strait Relations," *Seton Hall Journal of Diplomacy and International Relations* 18, no. 1, (Spring 2017), 55–71; Jing, "Xi Jinping's Taiwan Policy," 239–248.
4 Zhang Jie, "Do Not Think It Is Alarmist to Say 'When the Foundation Are Not Stable, the Earth Moves and the Mountains Shake,'" Taiwan.cn, March 7, 2016, http://www.taiwan.cn/plzhx/hxshp/zhzh/201603/t20160307_11403914 .htm; Qi Pengfei and Wang Fang, "On the Historical Legacy and Practical Significance of the Statement Concerning Taiwan-Related Issues in the 19th CPC National Congress Report," *Taiwan Studies*, no. 1 (2018), 1–12.
5 Chen Yiwen, "Tsai Ing-wen's Resolution of Cross-Strait Issue Mainland Scholars: Four Strategic Misperception," *China Times*, May 31, 2017, https:// www.chinatimes.com/cn/realtimenews/20170531002758-260407?chdtv.
6 On May 20, 2016, the spokesman of Taiwan Affairs Office of the State Council of PRC made this comment when he responded to the inauguration address of Tsai. See "Head of Taiwan Affairs Office of the State Council Comments on the Current Cross-Strait Relations," Taiwan Affairs Office of the State Council, May 20, 2016, http://www.gwytb.gov.cn/wyly/201605/ t20160520_11463128.htm.
7 "New Four No's" refers to the proposal made by Tsai on October 10, 2016, that "our pledges will not change, and our goodwill will not change. But we will not bow to pressure, and we will of course not revert to the old path of confrontation." See "President Tsai's 2016 National Day Address," Office of the President, October 10, 2016, https://english.president.gov.tw/News/4997. "Three New Ideas" refers to the proposal made by Tsai on May 3, 2017, which means "new situation, new test paper and new model." See Zhong Chenfang, "Tsai Ing-wen Proposes 'Three New Ideas' on Cross-Strait Relations," Voice of America, May 4, 2017, https://www.voachinese.com/a/tsai-new-approach -20170504/3836721.html
8 Matthew Strong, "Tsai Calls on DPP to Resist China Pressure," *Taiwan News*, September 29, 2016, https://www.taiwannews.com.tw/en/news/2986999.
9 Charles Hutzler and Jenny W. Hsu, "China Can't Make Taiwan 'Bow to Pressure,' Island's Leader Says," *Wall Street Journal*, October 4, 2016, https:// www.wsj.com/articles/china-cant-make-taiwan-bow-to-pressure-islands -leader-says-1475616782.
10 Zhang Xiaoyue, "We Will Definitely Not Accept the One China Principle," China Review Network, May 18, 2017, http://www.crntt.com/doc/1046/8/4/9 /104684945.html?coluid=93&kindid=8110&docid=104684945.

11 Sean Lin, "Lai Reaffirms Support for Independence," *Taipei Times*, September 27, 2017, http://www.taipeitimes.com/News/front/archives/2017/09/27/2003679217.

12 Amber Wang, "Taiwan 'Already Independent', Tsai Warns China," AFP (access from Yahoo News), January 15, 2020, https://news.yahoo.com/taiwan-already-independent-tsai-warns-china-062513557.html.

13 Zhong Yang, "Explaining National Identity Shift in Taiwan," *Journal of Contemporary China*, vol. 25, no. 99 (2016), 336–352; Xie Daning, "Syllabus, Identity and 'Cultural Taiwan Independence,'" *Taiwan Studies*, no. 1 (2017), 1–12.

14 Hao Dong and Dang Chaosheng, "Perspective on the Harm of 'Taiwan Independence Education,'" *Taiwan Studies*, no. 4 (2021), 61–69; "Taiwan Affairs Office of the State Council of PRC: Combine Chinese History as a Part of the East Asian History Curriculum Forcefully is a New Evidence of the Action of 'Taiwan Independence,'" Taiwan Affairs Office of the State Council of PRC, August 15, 2018, http://www.gwytb.gov.cn/wyly/201808/t20180815_12047573.htm.

15 Nyshka Chandran, "Donald Trump Insults China with Taiwan Phone Call and Tweets on Trade, South China Sea," *CNBC News*, December 5, 2016, https://www.cnbc.com/2016/12/05/donald-trump-insults-china-with-taiwan-phone-call-and-tweets-on-trade-south-china-sea.html; Yuan Zheng, "From Obama to Trump: Adjustments and Changes of Taiwan Policy of U.S.," *Taiwan Studies*, no. 2 (2017), 1–11.

16 Xi Jinping, "The Speech on the 40th Anniversary of the Publication of 'Message to Compatriots in Taiwan,'" Xinhua News Agency, January 2, 2019, http://www.xinhuanet.com/tw/2019-01/02/c_1210028622.htm.

17 David Axe, "U.S. Pacific Command Boss: The Chinese Military Is the 'Principal Threat,'" *National Interest*, February 14, 2019, https://nationalinterest.org/blog/buzz/us-pacific-command-boss-chinese-military-principal-threat-44497.

18 Xi Jinping, "Report at the Nineteenth National Congress of the CPC," *People's Daily*, October 28, 2017, http://cpc.people.com.cn/n1/2017/1028/c64094-29613660.html.

19 Brad Lendon, "Almost 40 Chinese Warplanes Breach Taiwan Strait Median Line; Taiwan President Calls It a 'Threat of Force,'" CNN, September 21, 2020, https://www.cnn.com/2020/09/21/asia/taiwan-china-warplanes-median-line-intl-hnk-scli/index.html.

20 "Foreign Ministry Spokesperson Wang Wenbin's Regular Press Conference on September 21, 2020," Ministry of Foreign Affairs of the People's Republic of China, September 21, 2020, https://www.fmprc.gov.cn/fyrbt_673021/jzhsl_673025/202009/t20200921_5419360.shtml.

21 Liu Xuanzun, "PLA Sent Nearly 200 Aircraft near Taiwan in Record Month," *Global Times*, November 1, 2021, https://www.globaltimes.cn/page/202111/1237849.shtml.

22 Huang Shunjie, "The First Version of 'the General Evaluation of National Defence' by the Tsai Administration: Taiwan Has Ability to Resist Enemies on the Other Side of the Strait," *United Morning Post*, March 17, 2017, http://www.zaobao.com/news/china/story20170317-736876.

23 Sean Lin, "Proposed Defense Budget to Rise 4.4%," *Taipei Times*, https://www.taipeitimes.com/News/front/archives/2020/08/14/2003741651.

24 Matt Yu and Matthew Mazzetta, "Taiwan Begins Construction of First Indigenous Submarine," ROC Central News Agency, November 24, 2020, https://focustaiwan.tw/politics/202011240017; Matt Yu and Joseph Yeh, "Taiwan's 1st Indigenous Landing Platform Dock a National Milestone: Tsai," ROC Central News Agency, April 13, 2021, https://focustaiwan.tw/politics /202104130011.

25 U.S. Department of Defense, "Report on Military and Security Developments Involving the People's Republic of China," November 4, 2021, https://media .defense.gov/2021/Nov/03/2002885874/-1/-1/0/2021-CMPR-FINAL.PDF.

26 Lin Yu-hsuan, Wang Yang-yu, and Joseph Yeh, "Taiwan Will Not be Forced into Talks by China: Defense Chief," ROC Central News Agency, November 5, 2021, https://focustaiwan.tw/cross-strait/202111050020.

27 ROC Central News Agency, "Taiwan President Tsai Ing-wen's National Day Speech (Full Text)," *Taiwan Times*, October 10, 2021, https://www.taiwannews .com.tw/en/news/4311090.

28 Wang Shushen, "The Trump Administration's Taiwan Policy and Its Implication," *The Chinese Journal of American Studies*, vol. 35, no. 5 (2021), 117–134.

29 "Trump's Ten Arms Sales to Taiwan, Military Rebalance in the Taiwan Strait," Institute for National Policy Research, http://inpr.org.tw/m/405-1728-8533 ,c111.php?Lang=en.

30 Matt Yu and Joseph Yeh, "Taiwan Makes Official Request to Buy New American Fighter Jets," Global Security, March 6, 2019, https://www.globalse-curity.org/wmd/library/news/taiwan/2019/taiwan-190306-cna01.htm?_m=3n %252e002a%252e2520%252eyo0ao00i7x%252e2bil.

31 Huizhong Wu and Johnson Lai, "Taiwan Deploys Advanced F-16V Fighter Jets amid China Threat," AP News, November 18, 2021, https://apnews.com/article /china-beijing-taiwan-tsai-ing-wen-3f3f4b8af3ae2d6679855be5e97f6f48.

32 Xin Qiang, "Enhancement of Security Cooperation between the US and the Taiwan Authority during the Trump Administration," *The Chinese Journal of American Studies*, vol. 35, no. 5 (2021), 102–116.

33 William Hetherington, "US Approves Submarine License," *Taipei Times*, April 8, 2018, http://www.taipeitimes.com/News/front/archives/2018/04/08 /2003690901.

34 Anthony Capaccio, "First Taiwan Arms Sale in Biden Administration Is Approved," *Bloomberg*, August 5, 2021, https://www.bloomberg.com/news /articles/2021-08-04/first-arms-sale-to-taiwan-by-biden-administration-is -approved.

35 "Taiwan Affairs Office of the State Council of PRC: Taiwan Should be Solely Responsible for Causing the Termination of Cross-Strait Communication Mechanisms," The State Council of PRC, June 29, 2016, http://www.gov.cn/ xinwen/2016-06/29/content_5086690.htm.

36 Chiu Bihui, "China vs. Taiwan – Controversy Over Flight Route M503," *DW News*, February 2, 2018, https://www.dw.com/en/china-vs-taiwan-contro-versy-over-flight-route-m503/a-42430594.

37 Finally, the two sides came to a compromise in which there would be two flights, with one flight by China Airlines of Taiwan and another by China Eastern Airlines of the mainland. On March 10 and 11, two charter flights evacuated a total of 361 Taiwanese stuck in Hubei Province back to Taiwan, with Taiwanese health staff on board to conduct quarantine procedures. See

Keoni Everington, "Taiwan Evacuates 361 on 2 flights from Wuhan, Those with Fevers Rejected," *Taiwan News*, March 11, 2020, https://www.taiwan-news.com.tw/en/news/3894937.

38 "Taiwan Affairs Office of the State Council Tells the Truth: The DPP Authorities Have Been Obstructing the Return of Taiwan Compatriots to Their Hometowns," Xinhua News Agency, February 15, 2020, http://www.xinhuanet.com/politics/2020-02/15/c_1125579458.htm.

39 Nicola Smith and Jonathan Pearlman, "Pacific Islands May Pivot to China, as Beijing Seeks to Isolate Taiwan," *Telegraph*, February 16, 2019, https://www.telegraph.co.uk/news/2019/02/16/pacific-islands-may-pivot-china-beijing-seeks-isolate-taiwan/.

40 Steve Lee Myers, "Taiwan Loses Nicaragua as Tensions with China Rises," *New York Times*, December 9, 2021, https://www.nytimes.com/2021/12/10/world/asia/taiwan-nicaragua-china.html. For the official statement from the Ministry of Foreign Affairs in Nicaragua, see Denis Moncada Colindres, "Nicaragua Recognizes the People's Republic of China as the Only Legitimate Government," Ministry of Foreign Affairs of Nicaragua, December 9, 2021, https://www.el19digital.com/articulos/ver/titulo:123654-nicaragua-reconoce-a-larepublica-popular-china-como-unico-gobierno-legitimo.

41 Keoni Everington, "Taiwan Ally Honduras Poised to Elect Pro-China Candidate," *Taiwan News*, November 12, 2021, https://www.taiwannews.com.tw/en/news/4342927.

42 Mimi Lau, "Caution at the Vatican amid US-China Tussle over Taiwan," *South China Morning Post*, October 13, 2021, https://www.scmp.com/news/china/diplomacy/article/3154287/caution-vatican-amid-us-china-tussle-over-taiwan.

43 Taipei rejoined the 2018 Kimberley Process annual meeting with the name "Chinese Taipei rough-diamond-trading entity" held in Belgium. See "Taiwan Rejoins the Diamond Trade's Kimberley Process," *Taipei Times*, November 20, 2018, http://www.taipeitimes.com/News/taiwan/archives/2018/11/20/2003704590.

44 Tong Liqun, "Overview of Taiwan Administration's External Relations in 2019," *Modern Taiwan Studies*, no. 1 (2020), 32–39.

45 "Mainland Opposes Foreign Intervention in Taiwan's Participation in Interpol Activities," *China Daily*, October 16, 2019, https://www.chinadaily.com.cn/china/2016-10/12/content_27040300.htm.

46 Shelley Shan, "Tourism Bureau Backed after Quitting Travel Show," *Taipei Times*, October 9, 2020, https://taipeitimes.com/News/front/archives/2020/10/09/2003744859.

47 "Press Conference on October 14, 2020," Taiwan Affairs Office of the State Council, October 14, 2020, http://www.taiwan.cn/xwzx/xwfbh/gtbxwfbh/fbhwb/202010/t20201014_12301209.htm.

48 The institutions of the Taiwan authorities in these countries are named "Republic of China (ROC)," except its office in Bahrain is named "Taiwan." Until July 13, 2019, the names of business institutions of Taiwan authorities in all aforementioned countries were renamed "Trade Representative Office of Taipei" as requested by host governments.

49 Zhao Juecheng, Du Haichuan, and Zhou Wei, "All the Foreign Airlines Rectified the Name before the Deadline, China Gave Affirmation to That," *Global Times*, July 26, 2018, http://world.huanqiu.com/exclusive/2018-07/12575296.html?agt=15438.

50 "Guyana Cancels Taiwan 'Office,'" *China Daily*, February 5, 2021, https://www.chinadaily.com.cn/a/202102/05/WS601cadfaa31024ad0baa776b.html.

51 "Foreign Ministry Spokesman Wang Wenbin Answers Reporters' Questions on the Letter from the Two Presidents of the EU Institutions to Some European Parliamentarians on Lithuania's Taiwan-Related Issues," Ministry of Foreign Affairs of the People's Republic of China, October 30, 2021, https://www.fmprc.gov.cn/web/fyrbt_673021/dhdw_673027/202110/t20211030_10404378.shtml.

52 Stan Hok-wui Wong and Nicole Wu, "Can Beijing Buy Taiwan? An Empirical Assessment of Beijing's Agricultural Trade Concessions to Taiwan," *Journal of Contemporary China*, vol. 25, no. 99 (2016), 353–371; Yi-Wen Yu, Ko-Chia Yu, and Tse-Chun Lin, "Political Economy of Cross-Strait Relations: Is Beijing's Patronage Policy on Taiwanese Business Sustainable?," *Journal of Contemporary China*, vol. 25, no. 99 (2016), 372–388.

53 Zhu Lei, "Current Status and Prospects of Cross-Strait Financial Exchanges and Cooperation," *Taiwan Studies*, no. 2 (2018), 49–54; Xue Yonghui, "Cross-Strait Judicial Assistance: Achievement and Challenges," *Taiwan Studies*, no. 3 (2018), 48–57.

54 Xi Jinping, "Report at the Nineteenth National Congress of the CPC."

55 Xi Jinping, "The Speech on the 40th Anniversary."

56 Li Keqiang, "Record of Premier Li Keqiang's Answers on Chinese and Foreign Press Conference," *Renmin Net*, March 15, 2019, http://npc.people.com.cn/n1/2017/0315/c14576-29147139-16.html.

57 Li Keqiang, "Premier Li Keqiang Attended the Press Conference and Answered Questions from Chinese and Foreign Journalists," Xinhua News Agency, March 12, 2021, http://www.xinhuanet.com/politics/leaders/2021-03/12/c_1127201014.htm.

58 Gunter Schubert, "China's 31 Preference Policies for Taiwan, an Opportunity, No Threat," Taiwan Insight, March 21, 2018, https://taiwaninsight.org/2018/03/21/chinas-new-31-preference-policies-for-taiwan-an-opportunity-no-threat/.

59 Xinhua News Agency, "Trade across Taiwan Strait Record High in 2018: Spokesperson," CGTN, January 16, 2019, https://news.cgtn.com/news/3d3d514e7759444d32457a6333566d54/index.html.

60 State Council of the People's Republic of China, "HK, Macao, Taiwan Residents Eligible for Residence Permit," August 16, 2018, http://english.www.gov.cn/state_council/ministries/2018/08/16/content_281476263616512.htm.

61 Yu Rou, "Taiwan Compatriots to Enjoy Preferential Treatment on Individual Income Tax: Spokesperson," Xinhua News Agency, December 26, 2018, http://www.xinhuanet.com/english/2018-12/26/c_137700400.htm.

62 For instance, Fujian Province introduced 66 preferential measures; Tianjin City, 52 measures; Zhejiang Province, 76 measures; Hubei Province, 62 measures; Xiamen City, 60 measures; Ningbo City, 80 measures.

63 Xinhua News Agency, "Mainland to Introduce More Preferential Policies for Taiwan Compatriots," *China Daily*, March 27, 2019, http://www.chinadaily.com.cn/a/201903/27/WS5c9b36e4a3104842260b2e9e.html.

64 Su Yung-yao and William Hetherington, "Beijing's New 26 Measures Condemned," *Taipei Times*, November 5, 2019, https://www.taipeitimes.com/News/front/archives/2019/11/05/2003725265; Nick Aspinwall, "Taiwan Rebukes Beijing's New 26 Measures for Cross-Strait Exchanges," *The Diplomat*,

November 9, 2019, https://thediplomat.com/2019/11/taiwan-rebukes-beijings -new-26-measures-for-cross-strait-exchanges.

65 "Overcome Difficulties, Promote Transformation, Welcome New Opportunities: '11 Measures' to Boost the Development of Taiwan-Funded Enterprises," Xinhua News Agency, August 20, 2020, http://www.xinhuanet.com/politics /2020-08/20/c_1126391308.htm.

66 Xinhua News Agency, "Taiwan Affairs Office of the State Council, Ministry of Agriculture and Rural Affairs, National Forestry and Grassland Administration and Other Departments Issued 'Several Measures to Support the Development of Taiwan Compatriots and Taiwan-Funded Enterprises in the Agricultural and Forestry Sector on the Mainland," Taiwan Affairs Office of the State Council, March 17, 2021, http://www.gwytb.gov.cn/zccs/zccs_61195/nl22t/202103/ t20210317_12338943.htm.

67 "Taiwan Affairs Office of the State Council: Various Departments around the 'Agriculture and Forestry 22 Measures' to Promote the Implementation of the Work Has Made Positive Progress," Taiwan Affairs Office of the State Council, May 12, 2021, http://www.gwytb.gov.cn/xwdt/xwfb/wyly/202105/t20210512 _12351719.htm.

68 "Taiwan Confirms China Has Not Ended Trade Agreement," *Taiwan News*, September 17, 2020, https://www.taiwannews.com.tw/en/news/4011107. Beijing officially announced in December 2021 that it will continue to implement ECFA from January 1, 2022. By the end of 2020, Taiwanese enterprises had benefited from the ECFA and enjoyed a cumulative tariff reduction of about $7 billion according to the information released by the TAO on December 29, 2021.

69 In 2016, the trade volume between the Chinese mainland and Taiwan was US$179.6 billion, down 4.5% from 2015. Mainland exports to Taiwan totaled US$40.4 billion, a 10.1% year-on-year drop, and imports from Taiwan stood at US$139.2 billion, down 2.8%. See "Cross-Strait Trade Down 4.5 pct in 2016," Xinhua News Agency, February 4, 2017, http://www.xinhuanet.com//english /2017-02/04/c_136031643.htm.

70 Xinhua News Agency, "Trade across Taiwan Strait Record High in 2018."

71 "Taiwan's Exports to Mainland Hit New High in 2020," Xinhua News Agency, January 9, 2021, http://www.xinhuanet.com/english/2021-01/09/c _139654465.htm.

72 Bonnie Glaser and Jeremy Mark, "Taiwan and China Are Locked in Economic Co-Dependence," *Foreign Policy*, April 14, 2021, https://foreignpolicy.com /2021/04/14/taiwan-china-econonomic-codependence.

73 Xinhua News Agency, "Cross-Strait Trade Saw Substantial Growth over Past Decade," January 27, 2022, http://www.china.org.cn/business/2022-01/27/ content_78013876.htm.

74 In 2016, when Tsai took office, Taiwan's exports to the mainland and Hong Kong accounted for 40.1% of its total exports. However, the dependence of Taiwan's exports on mainland China's market has been steadily increasing since then. In 2020, the figure was 43.9%, a historic record, and was 42.3% in 2021, despite Taipei's limitation policy and New South-Bound policy, even higher than the average figures of 39%–40% during Ma's administration.

75 "Cross-Strait Trade Down 4.5 pct in 2016," Xinhua News Agency.

76 "General Situation of Trade and Communication between Mainland and Taiwan in 2017," Ministry of Commerce of the PRC, March 1, 2018, http://tga .mofcom.gov.cn/article/sjzl/taiwan/201806/20180602760893.shtml.

77 "General Situation of Trade and Communication between Mainland and Taiwan in 2018," Ministry of Commerce of the PRC, January 18, 2019, http://tga.mofcom.gov.cn/article/sjzl/taiwan/201901/20190102828082.shtml.

78 Ministry of Commerce of PRC, "Statistics of Taiwan Investment in Mainland," Taiwan Affairs Office of the State Council of PRC, April 14, 2021, http://www.gwytb.gov.cn/local/201805/t20180525_11958860.htm.

79 Hua Xia, "Cross-Strait Trade Jumps 31.8 Percent in First Eight Months," Xinhua News Agency, September 15, 2021, http://www.news.cn/english/2021 -09/15/c_1310189777.htm#:~:text=BEIJING%2C%20Sept.,eight%20months %20of%20this%20year.

80 Ji Ye and Wang Shengmin, "From Reference to Foreign Investment to Equal Treatment: The Evolution and Limit of Taiwan Compatriots' Investment Treatment Standard," *Taiwan Research Journal*, no. 5 (2021), 38–47.

81 Cheng-hui Chen, "TSMC New Nanjing Fab to Ship Earlier than Expected," *Taipei Times*, December 11, 2017, http://www.taipeitimes.com/News/biz/ archives/2017/12/11/2003683759.

82 Zhu Lingqing, "Foxconn to Issue 1.97b Shares on Shanghai Stock Exchange," *China Daily*, May 14, 2018, http://www.chinadaily.com.cn/a/201805/14/WS5 af8f298a3103f6866ee82e3.html.

83 "Taiwan's Fubon Financial Holdings Takes a Stake in Xiamen Bank as a Direct Shareholder," Xinhua News Agency, December 12, 2018, http://www.xinhuanet.com/tw/2018-12/02/c_1123796545.htm.

84 "Taiwan Affairs Office of the State Council Introduced the Development of Cross-Strait Economic and Trade Cooperation," Taiwan Affairs Office of the State Council of PRC, September 15, 2021, http://www.gwytb.gov.cn/local /202109/t20210915_12378620.htm.

85 Financial Supervisory Commission of the ROC, "Cross-Strait Financial Business," September 29, 2021, https://www.fsc.gov.tw/en/home.jsp?id=353 &parentpath=0%2C5.

86 "Press Conference Series on January 16, 2019," Taiwan Affairs Office of the State Council, January 16, 2019, http://www.gwytb.gov.cn/xwdt/xwfb/fbh /201901/t20190116_12132541.htm. On July 30, 2019, Beijing declared to suspend the approval of the individual tourist application from all the 47 mainland cities, an action that will dramatically reduce the tourist numbers from the mainland to Taiwan.

87 "Anti-Infiltration Bill Is Tool to Ensure Tsai's Reelection," *China Daily*, January 1, 2020, https://global.chinadaily.com.cn/a/202001/01/WS5e0c83e3a 310cf3e35581e45.html.

88 Aside from Hong Kong and Macao, only 4 mainland cities among 61 cities, namely Beijing, Shanghai, Chengdu and Xiamen, are exempted from the suspension.

89 Xinhua News Agency, "Wang Yi, the Director of Taiwan Affairs Office of the State Council, Met with Mr. Hsieh Chang-ting on October 6, 2012 in Beijing," The Central People's Government of PRC, October 7, 2012, http://www.gov.cn /jrzg/2012-10/07/content_2238538.htm.

90 In the hierarchical government system of mainland China, Tianjin is a provincial-level city, while both Shenzhen and Xiamen are vice provincial-level cities.

91 Luo Wangshu, "Taichung Loses Right to Host 2019 Games," *China Daily*, July 26, 2018, http://www.chinadaily.com.cn/a/201807/26/WS5b59056ca31031a35

1e902a9.html; Teng Pei-ju, "Taichung Stripped of Right to Host East Asian Youth Games in Taiwan Due to Chinese Pressure," *Taiwan News*, July 24, 2018, https://www.taiwannews.com.tw/en/news/3489976.

92 "Press Conference Series on May 12, 2021," Taiwan Affairs Office of the State Council, May 12, 2021, http://www.gwytb.gov.cn/m/speech/202105/t20210512_12351716.htm.

93 "Deputy Director Liu Junchuan Delivers Speech at the 4th Seminar on 'National Reunification and National Revival,'" Taiwan Affairs Office of the State Council, October 30, 2021, http://www.gwytb.gov.cn/m/tbnews/202111/t20211102_12388303.htm.

94 "Taiwan Affairs Office of the State Council: Legal Punishment for Su Tseng-chang, You Shyi-kun, Joseph Wu and a Few Other 'Taiwan Independence' Stubborn Personnels," Taiwan Affairs Office of the State Council, November 15, 2021, http://www.gwytb.gov.cn/xwdt/xwfb/wyly/202111/t20211105_12389168.htm.

95 "Taiwanese Actor Dropped from Chinese Film after Political Outcry," *The Guardian*, July 15, 2016, https://www.theguardian.com/film/2016/jul/15/taiwanese-actor-dropped-china-no-other-love-independence.

96 "Press Conference Series on March 28, 2018," Taiwan Affairs Office of the State Council, March 28, 2018, http://www.gwytb.gov.cn/m/speech/201803/t20180328_11937824.htm.

97 Shih-ying Hsu and Jonathan Chin, "Taiwanese Film Banned from Chinese Theaters," *Taipei Times*, March 29, 2018, http://www.taipeitimes.com/News/front/archives/2018/03/29/2003690250.

98 "Press Conference Series on December 30, 2015," Taiwan Affairs Office of the State Council, December 30, 2015, http://www.gwytb.gov.cn/xwdt/xwfb/xwfbh/201512/t20151230_11345139.htm.

99 Zhang Zhijun, "It Is Intolerable for Taiwan Businessmen to Earn Money in Mainland while Supporting 'Taiwan Independence' When Coming Back," *Global Times*, December 2, 2016, https://taiwan.huanqiu.com/article/9CaKrnJYYmO.

100 Liang-sheng Lin and Jonathan Chin, "Hai Pa Wang Move Might Trigger 'one China' Domino Effect," *Taipei Times*, December 10, 2016, http://www.taipeitimes.com/News/taiwan/archives/2016/12/10/2003660927.

101 Stacy Hsu, "Amid Chinese Ire, 85°C Backs 'Consensus,'" *Taipei Times*, August 16, 2018, http://www.taipeitimes.com/News/front/archives/2018/08/16/2003698599.

102 "China Announced the Suspension of Imports of Taiwan Pineapples: The Council of Agriculture: Unacceptable," *Taiwan News*, February 26, 2021, https://www.taiwannews.com.tw/ch/news/4136942; Zhang Yi, "Taiwan's DPP Maliciously Misinterpreting Temporary Ban on Pineapple Imports," *China Daily*, March 1, 2021, https://www.chinadaily.com.cn/a/202103/01/WS603cea03a31024ad0baabf05.html.

103 Taiwan's Council of Agriculture complained that it just received the message at the same day of the official announcement of the ban on September 18, just one day before the ban took effect, without any cross-Strait prior consultation. See "Taiwan Threatens to Take China to WTO in New Spat over Fruit," *Reuters*, September 19, 2021, https://www.reuters.com/world/china/china-halts-taiwan-sugar-apple-wax-apple-imports-prevent-disease-2021-09-19.

104 "Mainland Slaps Punishment for Diehard Taiwan Secessionists; Detailed Measures Showcase Reunification Irresistible," *Global Times*, November 5, 2021, https://www.globaltimes.cn/page/202111/1238234.shtml.

105 "Taiwan Affairs Office of the State Council: Never Allow People Who Support 'Taiwan Independence' and Undermine Cross-Strait Relations to Make Money in the Mainland," Taiwan Affairs Office of the State Council, November 22, 2021, http://www.gwytb.gov.cn/xwdt/xwfb/wyly/202111/t20211122_12392201.htm.

106 It was reported that in 2016, when Su Chiao-hui was running for the seat in the Legislative Yuan, she received NT$2 million from the Far East Group, accounting for about 10% of donations for her campaign. In 2020, Far East Group donated NT$58 million for the legislator campaign; 69% went for DPP politicians. See "Taiwan's Far Eastern Group Got Fined in Mainland China, Accused of Being the Golden Master behind Su Tseng-chang," *United Morning Post*, November 22, 2021, https://www.zaobao.com.sg/realtime/china/story20211122-1216016.

107 "Taiwan Far East Group's Investment Enterprises in the Mainland Were Investigated and Punished for Violations of Laws and Regulations," Xinhua News Agency, November 22, 2021, http://www.news.cn/2021-11/22/c_1128086331.htm.

108 Xi Jinping, "Report at the Nineteenth National Congress of the CPC;" Xi Jinping "The Speech on the 40th Anniversary of the Publication of 'Message to Compatriots in Taiwan.'"

109 "Local Government Heads Arrive in Beijing for Talks," *Taipei Times*, September 18, 2016, http://www.taipeitimes.com/News/taiwan/archives/2016/09/18/2003655377.

110 As early as 2009, Kinmen county government had proposed to build a road bridge between Kinmen and Xiamen on the mainland. However, this proposal has been denied by Taipei. See Jiang Xun and Yuan Weijing, "Kinmen and Matsu Could Be Pioneers in Promoting Reunification, a New Variable of Cross-Strait Relations," *Asia Weekly*, March 10, 2019, http://theintellectual.net/zh/political/asia-weekly/1846-kinmen-and-matsu-to-promote-cross-strait-relations-unified-vanguard-of-the-latest-variable-xun-jiang-yuan-wei-jing.html; Nick Aspinwall, "6 Km from China, Taiwan's Kinmen Charts Its Own Path," *The Diplomat*, September 4, 2018, https://thediplomat.com/2018/09/6-km-from-china-taiwans-kinmen-charts-its-own-path/.

111 Zhang Yi, "Exchanges with Taiwan will Benefit 'One Family,'" *China Daily*, March 26, 2019, http://www.chinadaily.com.cn/a/201903/26/WS5c9964ada3104842260b278d.html.

112 Chai Baoyun and Zhang Xuan, "The Party Identification of Taiwan Voters and Its Influencing Factors: Analysis Based on the 'Nine in One' Election of Taiwan in 2014," *Taiwan Studies*, no. 1 (2018), 29–39; Yang Lixian, "A Close Look into the 'Ko Wen-je Phenomenon' and Its Impact on Taiwan's Party Politics," *Cross-Taiwan Strait Studies*, no. 3 (2015), 30–38.

113 Abraham Gerber, "Ko Wen-je Talks Colonialism, China," *Taipei Times*, February 1, 2015, http://www.taipeitimes.com/News/front/archives/2015/02/01/2003610545.

114 I-chia Lee, "Ko Adds Principle for Shanghai-Taipei Forum," *Taipei Times*, June 26, 2017, http://www.taipeitimes.com/News/taiwan/archives/2017/06/26/2003673324.

115 Alan Bairner, "2017 Taipei Universiade: The Political Power of Sport in Taiwan," *Taiwan Insight*, April 10, 2018, https://taiwaninsight.org/2018/04/10/2017-taipei-universiade-the-political-power-of-sport-in-taiwan.

116 "Shanghai-Taipei Signed a Number of Cooperation Memoranda," Taiwan.cn, December 21, 2018, http://www.taiwan.cn/xwzx/la/201812/t20181221_12124760.htm.

117 "The Full Text of Ko Wen-je's View about the Cross-Strait Relation," China Review Network, June 6, 2019, http://www.crntt.com/doc/1054/4/8/3 /105448393.html?coluid=0&kindid=0&docid=105448393.

118 "Press Conference Series on June 12, 2019," Taiwan Affairs Office of the State Council, June 12, 2019, http://www.gwytb.gov.cn/xwdt/xwfb/fbh/201906/ t20190626_12177651.htm.

119 "Ko Wen-je's Twin City Forum Speech: A Close Cross-Strait Family Is Better than a Hatred Family," China News Network, July 22, 2020, https://www.chi-nanews.com.cn/tw/2020/07-22/9244969.shtml.

120 "President Tsai Affirms Taiwan Will Not Accept 'One Country, Two Systems,'" Taiwan Today, January 3, 2019, https://taiwantoday.tw/news.php?post=148108 &unit=2.

121 Xi Jinping, "Report at the Nineteenth National Congress of the CPC."

122 "Zhang Zhijun Answered Questions to China Review Agency: To Promote the Process of Peaceful Reunification," China Review Network, March 5, 2017, http://www.crntt.com/doc/1045/9/8/3/104598324.html?coluid=3&kindid=13 &docid=104598324&mdate=0305210205.

4 Changes and continuity in mainland China's Taiwan policy

Introduction

The "Taiwan conundrum" has been regarded by mainland China as one of the most significant and vital issues for seven decades. The development of cross-Taiwan Strait relations had also witnessed quite a few astonishing turns and twists ever since 1949. After an eight-year discord between Beijing and Taipei under Chen Shuibian's administration, the cross-Strait relationship entered an unprecedented détente and charted into a "peaceful development" period from 2008 to 2016 during Ma Ying-jeou's administration. Nonetheless, the pendulum has swung the other way since Tsai Ingwen, candidate of the independence-leaning Democratic Progressive Party (DPP), won successive sweeping victories in the 2016 and 2020 presidential campaigns on the island. The friction across the Taiwan Strait not only resurfaced but, even worse, escalated.

For Beijing, acceptance and adherence to the one-China principle of Taipei is the anchor for cross-Strait peace and stability, and the foundation of mainland China's peaceful development policy. However, Beijing's repeated warnings that cross-Taiwan Strait relations would be fraught with disturbances without an explicit stance on the one-China principle have not been taken seriously in Taipei. Confronted by the consistent repudiation of the one-China principle by the Tsai administration, concerned by the DPP's "incremental Taiwan independence" maneuvers highlighted by the de-Sinicization process and proposals for "constitutional revision or interpretation," frustrated by the evident enhancement of US–Taiwan relations amid intensifying US-China hostility, and hobbled by the spiraling mutual distrust between the people of Taiwan and mainland China, Beijing began to make adjustments to its Taiwan policy from 2016 in accordance with the new situation across the Taiwan Strait.[1]

Turning from its eight-year peaceful development policy toward Taipei, Beijing responded forcefully to Tsai's steadfast refutation of the one-China

DOI: 10.4324/9781003163275-4

principle and was determined to ramp up multipronged pressure onto Taipei concentrating on security, political, and diplomatic arenas. The political stalemate continued after Beijing interrupted all of the official, quasi-official, and semiofficial cross-Strait communication channels since Tsai's inauguration. The international community witnessed the termination of an eight-year "diplomatic truce" and resumption of the "international space struggle" between the two sides. The encirclement of mainland military airplanes and warships around Taiwan island has become a regular operation of the People's Liberation Army (PLA). Correspondingly, it has triggered strong countermeasures from Taipei: it has invested massive resources to increase the military budget, endeavored to expand international space, purchased advanced weapons from the US, and strengthened US–Taiwan security cooperation. What is more, the mutual suspicion and populist rhetoric among both sides of the Strait are dramatically increasing.[2] However, contrary to Beijing's expectation, its hardline stance did not lead to Taipei's compromise; instead, it backfired due to Tsai's rebuke of the one-China principle and anti-engagement voices among Taiwanese people, which contributed to Tsai's resounding reelection victory, which in turn accelerated Beijing's anxiety.

Amid the extension of the impasse and the accumulation of tension, Beijing continued signaling to Taipei that it would neither tolerate any independence-leaning behaviors nor forsake the use of force. Beijing's statements, which included "preserving the option of taking all necessary measures," "not resigning to passing this problem on from one generation to the next," "unification is an inevitable requirement for the great rejuvenation of the Chinese nation," and the "historical task of the complete reunification of the motherland … will definitely be fulfilled," attracted broad attention both at home and abroad.[3] As a result, Admiral John Aquilino, then nominee to be commander of the Indo-Pacific Command, warned in March 2021 that Beijing was much closer than most people thought to consider military action against Taipei.[4] It also led to President Joe Biden's questionable pledge on October 21, 2021, to defend Taiwan in case of a mainland Chinese attack, and the reiteration by the US State Department that peace and stability across the Taiwan Strait are "central to the security and stability of the broader Indo-Pacific region and to the U.S."[5] Concerning the spike in cross-Strait tensions, Taiwan's Defense Minister Chiu Kuo-cheng proclaimed in October 2021 that, even though Taiwan would not "advance rashly" and set off a war with the mainland, Taipei would defend itself "full-on."[6] In addition to confirming US military presence on the island and claiming Taiwan is on the "front lines," Tsai also admitted that military threat from the mainland is increasing "every day."[7]

The aforementioned flexing of military muscle, accompanied by dueling rhetoric between Beijing and Taipei, has trapped the cross-Strait relationship in a "cold confrontation" featuring stinging security, political, and diplomatic struggles and plagued with severe setbacks since May 2016. Consequently, the world has witnessed a fundamental transition from peaceful development to an escalation of tension across the Taiwan Strait within the context of growing China–US strategic rivalry. Given that Beijing has consistently emphasized that acceptance of the one-China principle is the "unshakable foundation" of cross-Strait peace and stability, and considering how it has launched an intensifying pressure campaign against Taipei, a key question is whether these developments imply a profound deviation of the mainland's Taiwan policy from its conventional position, or more significantly, whether Beijing will resolve the Taiwan issue through force and lead the two sides to once again engage in armed conflict.

While the cross-Taiwan Strait relationship has been caught in a prolonged stalemate and experienced incessant turbulence in the past few years, it is undeniable that Beijing's Taiwan policy has demonstrated a certain conspicuous and fundamental continuity. In order to have a clear and precise understanding of the changes and continuity of Beijing's Taiwan policy, three key questions must be answered. First, what is the most prominent concern identified by Beijing that might make the mainland lose its patience and resort to using military force? Second, what is Beijing's underlying guideline for the final resolution of the Taiwan issue when Taipei does not want to accept reunification? And third, what is the strategic position of fulfilling reunification within Beijing's national grand strategic agenda?

Addressing the perpetuation of de facto independence: The change of Beijing's foremost concern

There is no doubt that deterring and containing Taiwanese independence, both de jure and de facto independence, is the top concern for Beijing's Taiwan policymakers. During the Lee Teng-hui and Chen Shui-bian administrations, Beijing succeeded in countering Taiwan's de jure independence moves by imposing multidimensional pressure. Nevertheless, after the DPP crushed the Kuomintang (KMT) in the 2016 presidential campaign and regained power, Beijing was alarmed by the ever-growing anti-reunification momentum in Taiwan, especially the tendency toward "maintaining de facto independence forever" given the risk of war. The overwhelming endorsement of the stance that "there is one China, and there is one Taiwan" and that "Taiwan is already an independent state under the name Republic of China" by the Taiwanese portrays a bleak outlook for reunification, the ultimate goal of Beijing. The mainland realized that compared with de jure independence, how to prevent de facto independence of Taiwan or the status quo of cross-Strait separation from being perpetuated has become a more prominent challenge to Beijing's reunification objective.

As continuously displayed by two decades of annual surveys conducted by the Mainland Affairs Council (MAC) of the Taiwan administration and Taiwan Chengchi University, generally speaking, less than 2% of Taiwanese want unification right away, less than 6% want immediate independence, and over 80% overwhelmingly prefer to maintain some version of the status quo. To a large extent, "no reunification at all" and "no independence right away (because of the risk of war)" have become the two "greatest common measures" for the majority of Taiwanese.[8] This combination of unwillingness to accept reunification with an unwillingness to risk pursuing formal independence has made maintaining the current de facto independence of Taiwan the most realistic and reasonable choice for the vast majority of Taiwanese (Figure 4.1).

The electoral system in Taiwan inevitably constrains the positions of both the KMT and the DPP, which means that neither of them will pursue and accept the reunification, or act it out in political practice. The KMT significantly deviated from its traditional one-China principle during the Lee administration. After Lee, whose "Two States Thesis" triggered a severe backlash from the mainland, KMT politicians gradually returned to endorse the "one China (ROC)" position, claiming that Taiwan is part of the Republic of China (ROC), based in Taipei, as defined by the ROC Constitution. However, the KMT displayed little interest in accepting the prospect of reunification across the Strait. Essentially, the KMT remains a pro-one-China party today but is by no means a pro-unification party. For example, President Ma Ying-jeou, an energetic advocate of the 1992 Consensus, pledged explicitly in his "Three No's" policy that there was no possibility for him to pursue reunification during his presidency. This also partly explains why the Ma administration did not resume the special institution the National Unification Council (*guojia tongyi weiyuanhui*), along with the Guidelines for National Unification (*guojia tongyi gangling*) "ceased" by the Chen administration in 2006.

After its astounding defeat by the DPP in the 2020 presidential election, the crestfallen KMT under the leadership of Johnny Chiang moved to alienate Beijing and downplay the role of the 1992 Consensus. In June 2020, a task force convened by the Kuomintang's Reform Committee issued new guidelines on cross-Strait relations and proposed that the consensus had lost its utility and should be replaced with a commitment to "upholding the Republic of China's national sovereignty."[9] Lin Wei-chou, the party whip of the KMT in Legislative Yuan, even suggested on October 10, 2020, to change the century-long official name of the Chinese Nationalist Party

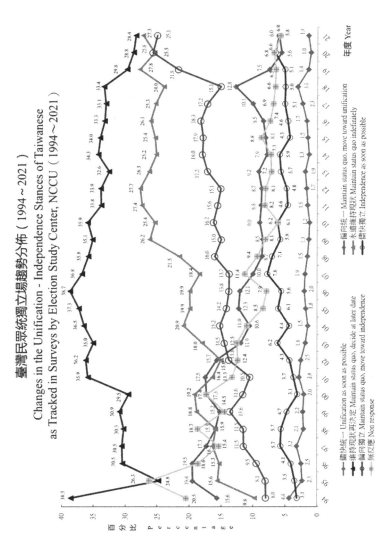

Figure 4.1 Changes in the unification–independence stances of Taiwanese as tracked in surveys by the Election Study Center, National Chengchi University (NCCU) (1994–2021). Source: Election Study Center of NCCU, https://esc.nccu.edu.tw/PageDoc/Detail?fid=7805&id=6962

(Kuomintang of China) to the Nationalist Party by removing "Chinese," in order to make the KMT a more Taiwan-centric party.[10] Expectedly, Beijing was enraged by the backtracking of the KMT on the one-China principle, leading to the dramatic cooling of the relationship between the Communist Party of China (CPC) and the KMT.

When Eric Chu Li-luan, a veteran politician who supports the 1992 Consensus and opposes Taiwan independence, unseated Johnny Chiang and won the chairmanship of the KMT in September 2021, Xi, in the name of general secretary of the CPC, issued a congratulatory letter calling for CPC–KMT cooperation for peace and reunification across the Strait. It is the first time that a mainland Chinese leader spoke of striving for "national unification" in a message to a leading KMT figure. In his reply, Eric Chu blamed the ruling DPP for being "anti-China," stated that "the people on both sides of the strait are both descendants of the Chinese," and pledged to increase mutual trust and integration, and strengthen exchanges and cooperation across the Strait. However, he did not touch upon the unification issue raised in Xi's message.[11]

On the flip side, as an adherent to the ultimate goal of Taiwanese independence, the DPP blames the ROC as a "foreign regime," or even an "invader" such as former colonist Japan. It views the totalitarian KMT regime as one that forcibly imposes the Chinese identity upon the Taiwanese people. As a victim of oppression from Chinese "outlanders," Taiwan must seek to establish a truly independent sovereign state under the leadership of the DPP. Based on that, the one-China principle is nothing but a trap for the Taiwanese, while the KMT is "an accomplice of the CPC" and a "traitor group" that is always trying to sabotage Taiwan's interests and betray Taiwan to the People's Republic of China (PRC). However, a series of behaviors pursuing the de jure independence of Chen, the first DPP president, led cross-Strait relations into a period of nail-biting turbulence. In light of the risk of advocating de jure independence, the DPP reluctantly switched to the stance of "maintaining the status quo" across the Strait, while still holding the banner of Taiwanese independence. For the DPP, there is no reason for Taiwan to accept the one-China principle because Taiwan and China (PRC) are two separate independent states, let alone consider the possibility of reunification.

A recent opinion poll conducted by the MAC of the Taiwan administration in November 2021 found that a total of 84.9% of Taiwanese want the island's present status to remain largely unchanged, while 85.5% oppose Beijing's "one country, two systems" formula. The notion that Taiwan and mainland China do not have a claim to each other's territory and that this situation amounts to the status quo found support among 77.7% of the respondents, while only 10.7% disagreed.[12]

According to Beijing, the "core contradiction" of cross-Strait relations ever since the 1990s has already changed from the "contradiction between the CPC and the KMT" to the "contradiction between reunification and Taiwan independence."[13] For Beijing, the widespread negative perception of the Taiwanese about the mainland and the overwhelming repudiation of reunification highlight the necessity of preparedness to deter not only de jure independence, but more importantly, the perpetuation of the de facto independence of Taiwan.

It is true that Beijing maintains sharp vigilance against the independence activists in Taiwan who are attempting to detach Taiwan "legitimately" from China by various means, including drawing up a new constitution, amending or interpreting the constitution, or holding a referendum on independence. However, after more than a decade of wrestling with the Lee and Chen administrations, Beijing has established a restrictive framework, culminating in the passage of the Anti-Secession Law in March 2005, to effectively deter Taipei's de jure independence attempts. It contributed to Chen's reluctant recognition that Taiwanese independence was "impossible" when his brinkmanship led him to be labeled as a "troublemaker" by both Beijing and Washington.[14] It also explains the self-restraint of advocating de jure independence after the DPP resumed the presidency in 2016. Even though the DPP simultaneously obtained an absolute majority in the legislature, the Tsai administration adopted a policy implying one-China ambiguously by touching upon the ROC Constitution, ROC constitutional order, and the Act Governing Relations Between the People of Taiwan Area and the Mainland Area, instead of moving radically toward de jure independence, which would have infuriated Beijing.

Based on the continuous expansion of the power asymmetry across the Taiwan Strait, Beijing has become more confident that it has sufficient capability and policy leverages to deter Taipei from achieving de jure independence. What concerns Beijing most is not to contain de jure independence, which is only possible in theory, but to oppose any practical measures that might be taken by the Taiwan administration leading to the irreversible perpetuation of the de facto independence of Taiwan. Concretely speaking, Beijing has kept a closer watch on three types of strengthening momentums conducive to that scenario.

The first momentum is the advocacy of "Independent Taiwan" (*dutai*) policies and political narrative that "Taiwan is already a sovereignty independent state," which has no relevance to China. In contrast with the KMT, which still sticks to the position that "both the Mainland and Taiwan belong to the ROC," DPP politicians insist that the "ROC is Taiwan," and actually the "ROC is none other than Taiwan," therefore, the relationship between Taiwan and the mainland is a relationship between two sovereign independent states, instead of two separate areas within one state. For example, in May 2019, the Legislative Yuan, controlled by the DPP, passed an amendment to the Criminal Code, treating people from the mainland, Hong Kong, and Macau as "foreigners." This behavior was regarded by Beijing as a new attempt to legalize and institutionalize the DPP's position of "one China, one Taiwan" via legislation. Furthermore, according to DPP's discourse, Taiwan, with the name of ROC presently, is already "a sovereign and independent state" that does not need to take the risk to declare independence at all. For example, in her first interview four days after her reelection in January 2020, Tsai told the BBC explicitly that there was "no need" to formally announce independence because "we are an independent country already and we call ourselves the Republic of China, Taiwan."[15] Unification between the two sides would be no more "reunification" of a state, but constitute the "invasion" and "annexation" of Taiwan as a sovereign state by another sovereign state, China. General recognition of such a political stance will make it impossible for Taiwan to accept reunification at any time, in any form, for any reason.

Beijing's second anxiety comes from the ever-deepening de-Sinicization process in social, cultural, and educational areas, initiated by Lee and promoted by the DPP, including the revision of history textbooks, demonization of the KMT's governance, as well as whitewashing of the colonial domination of the Japanese Empire in Taiwan's modern history.[16] One of the most recent examples is the disputable revision of a middle school history textbook. As early as when Lee was in office, he began to advocate the so-called concentric circle historical view, which termed mainland China as simply a part of East Asia, without historical relations with Taiwan. In November 2006, Chen put forward a revised guideline for the textbook that separated "Taiwanese history" from "Chinese history," aiming to establish a historical view that "Taiwan has always been an independent state but was invaded and controlled successively by China, the Netherlands and Japan." At the end of his second term, Ma tried to make a few minor adjustments to the high school curriculum, including changing the term of "governance of Japanese Empire" back to "occupation of Japanese Empire" and indicating that thousands of women were "compelled to be" comfort women during the World War II. Yet his efforts failed when the High School Curriculum Review Commission, under the Tsai administration, decided to block the implementation of the Ma-proposed curriculum. Furthermore, Tsai's administration required that Chinese history should not be taught anymore as an independent course, but as part of the East Asian history curriculum. The ultimate purpose of Taipei's de-Sinicization efforts is to cut off the historical and cultural connection with China and establish an exclusive Taiwanese identity by teaching that Taiwanese history is not part of Chinese history. By asserting that Taiwanese culture is not a part of Chinese culture and that Taiwanese is not Chinese, their aim is to pave the way for peaceful and eternal separation between two different and irrelevant "states" across the Strait. The aforementioned maneuvers advocated by both KMT and DPP pro-independence politicians, defined by Beijing as "creeping independence behaviors" (*yinxing taidu*), constitute the greatest challenge to cross-Strait relations.[17] This concern has precipitated Xi's proclamation of the "Six Any's" (*liuge renhe*) message on November 11, 2016, that Beijing "will never allow anyone, any organization or political party to rip out any part of our territory at any time or in any form."[18] In his opening speech at the 19th National Congress of the CPC, Xi again emphasized the PRC's sovereignty over Taiwan, stating that Beijing has sufficient abilities to "thwart any form of Taiwan independence attempts."[19]

The third momentum concerns the ever-strengthening relations between the US and Taiwan administration, within the context of a China–US strategic adversary. The Taiwan issue has always been intertwined with the fluctuation of China–US relations. To a certain degree, US compliance with its one-China policy and non-support to Taiwanese independence has historically contributed to the mainland's confidence and patience to pursue a policy of peaceful reunification.[20] However, the notable progress in the US–Taiwan relations since President Donald Trump took office made Beijing worry that Washington intended to play the Taiwan issue as a geopolitical card as the China–US strategic rivalry grew increasingly intense.[21] Beijing was startled by the unprecedented phone call between Trump and Tsai in December 2016, and Trump's implication that a break from the one-China policy, the backbone of US–China relations for decades, was possible. Washington's support for Taipei's "maintaining status quo" policy and the multidimensional improvement of US–Taiwan relations further placed Beijing on alert.[22] For instance, the frequent arms sales of advanced weapon systems, such as the F-16V jet fighters and M1A2 main battle tanks, MQ-9 SeaGuardian drones, tactical ballistic missiles, long-range cruise missiles, and land-based anti-ship missiles, ignited military counterattacks from Beijing. The introduction and passage of a series of pro-Taiwan acts, including the Taiwan Travel Act in 2018 and the TAIPEI Act in 2020,[23] were interpreted by Beijing as an effort to "normalize" US–Taiwan political and defense relations.[24] Additionally, the successive port calls of US naval research vessels in Taiwan's Kaohsiung City and Keelung City, the proposal to rename the Washington-based Taipei Economic And Cultural Representative Office to the Taiwan Representative Office, the joint humanitarian rescue exercise in the southern Pacific, declassification of the Six Assurances and inclusion of it in the US one-China policy package, as well as the public meeting between the chiefs of National Security Council of the US and Taiwan, ignited Beijing's suspicions that Washington sought to compromise its one-China policy in order to check and balance the rise of China.

Given the deterioration of US–China relations after China was defined as a fundamental and long-term adversary by the US, Beijing believes Washington is trying to promote the US–Taiwan security relationship to a "quasi-alliance" and help to defend Taipei's de facto independence so as to retain the peaceful separation across the Strait as long as possible. The emerging US–Taiwan alignment, featuring active political coordination and military cooperation, will further strengthen Taipei's adherence to its policy of maintaining de facto independence and embolden Taipei to resist any appeal of reunification from the mainland (Figure 4.2 and Table 4.1).

After Trump's departure from office, President Biden continues to set off alarm bells in Beijing. On August 19, 2021, when President Biden was interviewed by ABC, he suggested the US would come to defend Taiwan

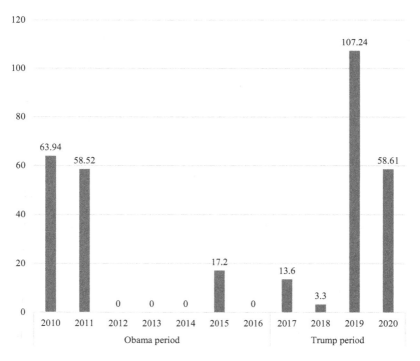

Figure 4.2 U.S. arms sales to Taiwan from Obama to Trump era (per US$100 million).

Table 4.1 U.S. arms sales to Taiwan from Obama to Trump era (per US$100 million)

Year	Obama period							Trump period			
	2010	2011	2012	2013	2014	2015	2016	2017	2018	2019	2020
Amount	63.94	58.52	0	0	0	17.2	0	13.6	3.3	107.24	58.61
Total				139.66						183.35	

Sources: FMS Data from the Defense Security Cooperation Agency, https://www.dsca.mil; Taiwan Defense and National Security, Taiwan Arms Sales Notified to Congress, 1990–2020, https://www.ustaiwandefense.com/taiwan-arms-sales-notified-to-congress-1990-2020.

in the event of a mainland attack by comparing its Taiwan commitments to those in NATO.[25] It was immediately applauded by Taipei as the "clearest declaration about 'defending Taiwan' since Joe Biden took office."[26] Beijing was surprised again by the statement made by President Biden, during a CNN town hall on October 22, 2021, that the US has "a commitment" to come to Taiwan's defense if mainland China were to attack.[27] Although a White House official shortly attempted to clarify Biden's comments on Taiwan, saying the president was "not announcing any change in our policy and there is no change in our policy" in his remarks about cross-Strait relations,[28] Beijing had enough reason to question whether these statements were simply slips of the tongue or reflected the true intention of Biden's administration concerning the Taiwan issue. On October 26, 2021, US Secretary of State Antony Blinken issued a statement claiming that "Taiwan's meaningful participation in the UN system is not a political issue, but a pragmatic one" and "encourage all UN Member States to join us in supporting Taiwan's robust, meaningful participation throughout the UN system."[29] Beijing, outraged by this new measure seeking to create and legalize "two Chinas" or "one China, one Taiwan" in the international arena, warned it would "definitely" cause "subversive and enormous risks" to China–US relations.[30]

For Beijing, it appears that maintaining the status quo of Taiwan's de facto independence has already become the common goal of the US and the two major parties in Taiwan. Washington's pro-Taiwan policy confirmed Beijing's built-up suspicion that the objective of the US is to permanently detach Taiwan from the mainland by collusion with Taipei. Additionally, both the KMT and the DPP intend to equate the ROC with Taiwan in political practice and reject reunification across the Strait. The only difference between them is that the KMT is satisfied with preserving the current political split permanently under the name ROC or ROC (Taiwan), while the DPP still intends to "transform" the ROC gradually into the ROC Taiwan, then the Republic of Taiwan through "Taiwanization" of the ROC by the "localization process" (*bentuhua*) and "rectification campaign" (*zhengming yundong*).[31] The reiteration of "ROC Taiwan" by Tsai in her speech on October 10, 2021, therefore, provoked ire from Beijing.

However, for Beijing, whose ultimate goal is to fulfill reunification, any attempt to maintain Taiwan's de facto independence indefinitely under the name ROC is nothing more than "a disguised type of Taiwan independence" (*bianxiang taidu*). As "The One-China Principle and the Taiwan Issue" white paper stated, one of the three conditions for the mainland to use force is if "the Taiwan authorities refuse, *sine die*, the peaceful settlement of cross-Straits reunification through negotiations."[32] It sent a clear signal to Taipei that Beijing will not tolerate the indefinite postponement of political negotiation steering to reunification. The Anti-Secession Law also enunciated that Beijing shall employ "non-peaceful means and other necessary measures" if the "possibilities for a peaceful reunification should be completely exhausted." The afore-quoted proclamation reflected the mainland's worry about Taiwan's permanent separation, either by an overt move to de jure independence or particularly by continued refusal to unify with the Chinese mainland.

The political and social change on the island manifested by the victory of the DPP in 2016 reinforced Beijing's concerns. Subsequently, Xi reemphasized that Beijing will never allow the split of China "in any form," which implies that if Taipei adopts "delaying tactics" to maintain the cross-Strait separation forever and repudiate reunification for an indefinite period, Beijing will have to resort to the use of force to fulfill reunification.[33] In his May 2020 speech marking the 15th anniversary of the implementation of the Anti-Secession Law, Li Zhanshu, chairman of the National People's Congress (NPC) of the PRC, warned that "'Taiwan independence' is a path to nowhere" and Beijing is "willing to create vast space for peaceful reunification, but we will definitely not leave any room for separatist activities aimed at 'Taiwan independence' in any form."[34]

Furthermore, concerning the insistence by Washington and Taipei on maintaining the status quo, which is regarded by Beijing as a cloak for the pursuit of permanent separation across the Strait, the mainland started to define "status quo" in its own way. In light of the challenge of the US to the UN Resolution 2758 and constant blame upon Beijing of "unilaterally changing the status quo," President Xi drove home to President Biden in the 2021 virtual meeting that

> the true status quo of the Taiwan question and what lies at the heart of one China are as follows: there is but one China in the world and Taiwan is part of China, and the Government of the People's Republic of China is the sole legal government representing China.[35]

It is the first time that mainland China's top leader gave an explicit definition of the cross-Strait status quo.

'Placing more hope on the mainland itself': Beijing's strategic guideline to promote reunification

Since the split of the two sides across the Taiwan Strait in 1949, Beijing's strategic guideline to engage Taipei and promote reunification has witnessed several significant transformations. At the very beginning, Beijing tried to promote reunification by "placing hope on the Taiwan administration" when

Taiwan was under the one-party rule of the KMT. With the political changes in Taiwan, the mainland thereafter switched to the guideline of "placing more hope on Taiwanese people" and extended an olive branch to Taiwan by strengthening economic, social, and cultural exchanges. Nevertheless, this approach falters against a background in which the majority of Taiwanese oppose the prospect of reunification. In this context, the feasibility of the primary guideline of placing hope on Taiwanese people was severely challenged. To the present day, although still claiming to place hope on the Taiwanese, Beijing has adjusted further to "place more hope on mainland China itself" as the underlying doctrine to promote reunification.

When Taiwan was under the firm control of the KMT alone during the Chiang Kai-shek and the Chiang Ching-kuo administrations, Beijing tried to prompt Taipei to mutually pursue reunification by essentially "placing hope on the KMT administration."[36] Beijing knew clearly that both Chiang Kai-shek and Chiang Ching-kuo were steadfast adherents of the one-China principle and implacable opponents of Two Chinas and Taiwanese independence. Based on this common understanding, Chairman Mao suggested in January 1956 that "the CPC and the KMT had already cooperated twice, now we are ready for the third time cooperation."[37] Amid the second Taiwan Strait Crisis in August 1958, Beijing issued a "Second Message to Compatriots in Taiwan" and called for direct peace talks between the CPC and the KMT, whereupon the two sides could "turn from enemies to friends."[38] It also explained the confidence of Mao when he told Dr. Henry Kissinger in 1973 that Beijing was willing to "wait for a hundred years" concerning the Taiwan issue.[39]

After Chiang Ching-kuo became the president of the ROC in May 1978, Beijing began to explicitly encourage him to carry out the third CPC–KMT cooperation by conducting party-to-party negotiations on a reciprocal basis.[40] On June 26, 1983, Deng stated again that since "peaceful reunification has become the common language of the CPC and the KMT," the "appropriate way for the realization of peaceful reunification is to hold CPC–KMT talks on an equal footing" and bring about "the third cooperation between the two parties."[41] Lee Teng-hui, who inherited the presidency in January 1988, repeatedly announced that "there is only one China, not two" and that "China should be reunited," encouraging Beijing to continue its active engagement policy with the Lee administration. The first Wang–Koo meeting, held in Singapore in April 1993, was regarded as an aspiring symbol of the political détente across the Strait. However, after successfully consolidating his power and purging the other KMT patriarch, Lee gradually turned to preach "two reciprocal political entities" and remarked "Taiwan is already a state with independent sovereignty."[42] Lee's visit to the US in June 1995, and his "Two States Thesis" in July 1999, ignited strong countermeasures from Beijing.[43] The victory of the DPP's Chen Shuibian in the 2000 presidential campaign led Beijing to realize that the guideline of placing hope on the KMT administration had to be changed. Moreover, since taking power in May 2000, Chen consistently trumpeted the ideology of Taiwanese independence by propagating "Taiwan and China are one country at each side (of the Taiwan Strait)," proposing a referendum on "seeking membership in the United Nations under the name Taiwan" and "constitutional amendments or revision."[44] Correspondingly, Beijing adopted a no-contact policy and ratcheted up pressure against Chen's advocacy of pro-independence activities.[45]

From the mid-1990s to 2008, the intensifying cross-Strait tensions drove Beijing to close the door to engagement with the Lee and Chen administrations, consequently making it impossible to continue with its guideline of placing hope on the Taiwan administration. Thereafter, Beijing began to shift toward placing more hope on the Taiwanese people to promote reunification. For example, concerned by the emerging pro-independence signs of Lee, Jiang's "Eight-Point Proposal," revealed on January 30, 1995, explicitly stated that "more hope will be pinned on the Taiwanese compatriots while still pinning hope on the Taiwanese authorities."[46] In March 2005, Hu reiterated in his "Four-Point Proposal" that the mainland would "never change the principle of placing hope on the Taiwan people," and "always respect, trust and rely on" the Taiwanese people "under whatever circumstances."[47] This doctrine was succeeded and echoed by President Xi as he claimed that Beijing would "remain committed to the principle of placing our hopes on the people of Taiwan" in his January 2019 speech.[48]

Fair to say, the idea of placing hope on the Taiwanese people is not the indigenous innovation of President Jiang. As early as the issuance of the "Message to Compatriots in Taiwan" in January 1979, Beijing had already declared that it would "place hope on 170 million Taiwan people as well as the Taiwan administration."[49] However, Beijing had for decades pursued the fulfillment of reunification by conducting political dialogue with the KMT administrations.[50] Before the Lee administration, the idea of placing hope on the Taiwanese had not been substantially implemented as a concrete and effective policy. Since cross-Strait relations hit rock bottom during the Lee and Chen administrations, Beijing has begun to introduce a sequence of policies, regulations, and measures to engage ordinary Taiwanese people in order to win their hearts and minds. After Ma Ying-jeou assumed the presidency in May 2008, Beijing successfully fulfilled the direct and two-way links of mail service, transport, and trade, and reached a bunch of agreements ranging from economic integration, tourist interflow, and financial coordination, to cultural and social exchanges.[51] The official interaction between the two sides reached a climax during the historic Xi–Ma Summit in November 2015. With the unprecedented and comprehensive progress in the political, economic, and social arenas, Beijing grew far more optimistic about the prospect of reunification and the effect of its guideline of placing more hope on the Taiwanese people when cross-Strait relations navigated into a historical peace and development stage.

However, Beijing's fleeting optimism was dealt a heavy blow by the domestic political and social reaction within Taiwan. Contrary to Beijing's expectations, its accommodative and cooperative policies toward Taipei had not induced the Taiwanese people to welcome the prospect of reuni-fication. Take the Cross-Strait Service Trade Agreement signed by Beijing and Taipei in June 2013 as an example. For Beijing, this agreement displayed its goodwill to the Taiwanese people by providing a more favorable arrangement and condition to the Taiwan side. However, fear that this agreement would place Taiwan's economic security and political autonomy at risk triggered large-scale protests led by students, namely, the Sunflower Movement in March 2014. Beijing was bedeviled by the controversy and contention concerning the ratification of the agreement. A poll conducted in 2016, when Tsai began her first presidential campaign, showed that 64% of Taiwanese were skeptical of cross-Strait economic cooperation and worried that the mainland would attempt to force Taiwan to accept political concessions due to growing economic interdependence.[52] The overwhelming mistrust among the Taiwanese about the cross-Strait economic integration engineered by the mainland was reflected in the crushing defeat of the Beijing-friendly KMT in local elections in November 2014 and the presidential campaign in January 2016, driving Beijing to reexamine the effectiveness of its guideline of placing hope on Taiwanese people.

Additionally, what concerned Beijing more was the continuous evaporation of Chinese identity and the rising of anti-mainland sentiment among the Taiwanese. In accordance with the guideline of placing hope on Taiwanese people, Beijing has always kept an eye on fluctuations in public opinion among the Taiwanese toward the mainland, especially regarding national and state identity issues.[53] In 1992, when the two sides prepared for the Wang–Koo meeting, around 25.5% of Taiwan's residents identified themselves exclusively as Chinese, while 17.6% identified as exclusively Taiwanese, and 46.4% said both Chinese and Taiwanese. However, since then, Taiwan residents have increasingly identified themselves as Taiwanese rather than Chinese, especially after Taiwan morphed into a democracy in the late-1990s. In 2016, in the aftermath of the Sunflower Movement, only 3.4% still identified themselves exclusively as Chinese, and more than 58% were Taiwanese. The figures have remained consistent ever since. By December 2019, only 38% of Taiwan's residents thought of themselves as either Chinese (3.3%) or as both Chinese and Taiwanese (34.7%). A survey released by National Chengchi University's Election Study Center showed that in 2020 self-identification as Taiwanese and Chinese, or solely as Chinese has dropped to record lows, while 64.3% of the public regard themselves as Taiwanese. Respondents identifying as both Taiwanese and Chinese dropped to 29.9%, while those identifying solely as Chinese fell to 2.6%.[54] What is more, Taiwan's demographic trajectory implies that as time passes, the continuation of this trend will make a solely Taiwanese identity prevail as the consensus of residents, subsequently further weakening the willingness of the Taiwanese to accept reunification (Figure 4.3).

Disillusioned by widespread anti-mainland sentiment and increasingly distrustful views toward closer cross-Strait relations among the Taiwanese, Beijing was forced to conclude that the fulfillment of reunification can neither rely simply on the Taiwan administration nor the Taiwanese people. Instead, it has to fall back on the political determination of the mainland for reunification based on its comprehensive development. In others words, Beijing must place more hope on the mainland itself. President Xi reinforced this point on March 5, 2015, stating that "fundamentally, the vital and decisive element for the future direction of cross-strait relations is the development and progress of mainland China itself."[55] On November 6, 2020, Liu Jieyi, minister of the Taiwan Affairs Office (TAO), also pointed out that "development and progress of the motherland is a key factor in determining the direction of cross-Strait relations and leading the process of national rejuvenation."[56]

The adoption of this self-reliant guideline means that although Beijing will still try its best to appeal to the Taiwanese to embrace reunification by implementing multidimensional favorable and beneficial measures, Beijing's Taiwan policy shall not be diverged or distorted by the domestic politics of Taiwan, including party alternation, social movements, the flow of public opinion, and the rise and fall of political powers. In adherence to its ultimate goal, the initiative, timetable, roadmap, approaches, and measures for achieving reunification will and must be determined by Beijing, instead of Taipei. In the most recently released Communique of the Sixth Plenary Session of the CPC Central Committee in November 2021, Beijing reaffirmed that it "will firmly maintain the leadership and initiative in cross-Straits relations."[57]

Strategically, it implies that Beijing will persistently focus on self-development, thereby irreversibly enlarging the comprehensive power asymmetry across the Strait as time elapses. Consequently, the power margin of the mainland over Taiwan will equip Beijing with more powerful policy instruments to deter Taipei's pro-independence venture and make reunification a more attractive goal to the Taiwanese. When the mainland began to formally pursue a peaceful reunification policy in 1979, the gross domestic

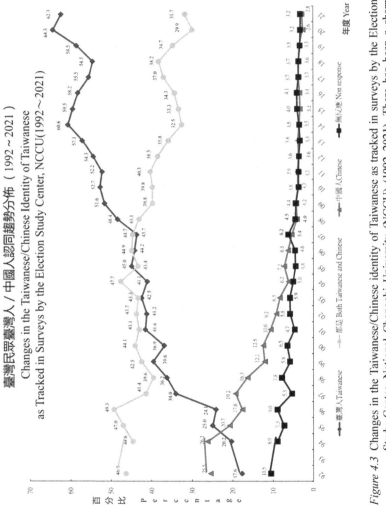

Figure 4.3 Changes in the Taiwanese/Chinese identity of Taiwanese as tracked in surveys by the Election Study Center, National Chengchi University (NCCU) (1992–2021). There has been a sharp increase in Taiwanese identity and a salient decrease in Chinese identity. Source: Election Study Center of NCCU, https://esc.nccu.edu.tw/PageDoc/Detail?fid=7804&id=6960.

product (GDP) of the mainland was US$178 billion, while Taiwan was US$33.8 billion, about five times larger. In 1987, when the two sides started exchanges, the GDP of the mainland was US$272 billion, just three times larger than Taiwan whose GDP was US$105 billion. However, in 2021, the GDP of the mainland was US$17.7 trillion, about 22 times Taiwan's GDP, which was about US$773 billion. Even though it is expected that the annual growth rate might drop to 6%–7% per year in the near future, the incremental GDP of the mainland would equal 1.5 of Taiwan's GDP every year. At the same time, the development of an industrial–scientific–technological infrastructure on the mainland provides a strong engine for the expansion of the PLA's capability. In 2021, the military budget of the PLA was about US$252 billion, which is about 21 times Taiwan's US$12 billion. The PLA's incremental budget was the equivalent of Taiwan's annual defense expenses. It is clear that Beijing is more confident than before that "time is on its side," especially in terms of the "hard power" growth trajectory. Such confidence contributed to the proclamation in a pivotal resolution, the third-ever such resolution in the 100-year history of the CPC, that "for realizing China's complete reunification, time and momentum are always on our side."[58]

Tactically, it suggests that Beijing will more readily be able to apply pressure upon any Taiwan administration that does not explicitly accept the one-China principle. It is undeniable that for decades, Beijing has been baffled by the carrot-and-stick dilemma, since it understands that a hardline policy will lead to anti-China emotion among the Taiwanese, which will not be conducive toward winning the hearts and minds of the Taiwanese people to embrace reunification. However, this self-reliant guideline of placing hope on the mainland itself implies Beijing will not be so passive and instead will be more willing to pursue a strong-arm policy and bear the resulting cost. It explained the recent unilateral suspension of individual tourist permission, implementation of the fruit exportation ban, introduction of a die-hard secessionist list, and punishment of important donors or "paymasters" to the DPP. Profoundly disappointed by the consecutive overwhelming victories of the DPP in the 2016 and 2020 election campaigns, growing anti-China sentiment and the emergence of a "natural independent (*tianran du*) generation," the mainland in the foreseeable future will pay comparatively less attention to the negative responses from the Taiwanese public, and employ tougher measures with less hesitation to counter any independence-leaning maneuvers on the part of Taipei.

Concerning the current security standoff and political deadlock across the Strait, it is evident that Beijing still hopes to resume official communication and political interaction with Taipei on the basis of the one-China principle.[59] Nevertheless, a series of actions taken by Taipei around the election, including the enactment of the Anti-Infiltration Act, amendments of five laws relating to national security, the initiation of a referendum on a "framing constitution" by the pro-independence deep-green wing, and the introduction of legislation to rename the passport and China Airlines company, has led Beijing to believe there is little hope of avoiding more turbulent cross-Strait relations in the future.

The stinging interaction between the two sides involving the COVID-19 pandemic provides a remarkable example of the extent to which cross-Strait relations have deteriorated. Contrary to the common expectation, the COVID-19 pandemic unexpectedly became a catalyst for worsening cross-Strait relations. Even though Beijing agreed to receive Taiwan's medical experts to conduct a field investigation in Wuhan, the epicenter of the global pandemic in its early stages, and did not oppose the participation of Taiwanese officials in weekly online video conferences organized by the World Health Organization (WHO), Beijing was incensed at Taipei's persistent labeling of the coronavirus as the "Wuhan Virus," an export ban on facial masks to the mainland, and a dispute regarding charter flights to facilitate the return of Taiwanese living in Hubei Province to Taiwan. For Beijing, it was the DPP administration that made a mockery of even humanitarianism efforts by scorning Beijing, scoffing at Wuhan, and utilizing the outbreak to hit out at the mainland at a time when mainland Chinese people was struggling to control the spread of the deadly virus. Furthermore, Beijing was alerted by Taipei's energetic efforts to take part in the World Health Assembly – seen by Taiwan as an opportunity to expand its international leverage without adhering to the one-China principle in the shadow of the pandemic. Consistent support from Washington to Taipei, exemplified by the signing of the US–Taiwan joint statement on combating COVID-19, aggravated Beijing's suspicion that Taipei was looking forward to taking advantage of the US–China rivalry and contriving to "pursue independence through 'pandemic diplomacy'" (*yiyi moudu*). Although Beijing understood that blocking Taipei's participation in the WHA would lead to a fierce backlash from the Taiwanese and inflame anti-China emotion on the island, it still called on the WHO not to issue an invitation letter to Taipei because of Tsai's refutation of the one-China principle. In other words, Beijing has prepared itself to persist with its pressure-imposing policy and bear any costs that result from it.

Modernization first: The relation between reunification and national rejuvenation

For the mainland, the split across the Taiwan Strait is a lingering issue leftover from the 100-year humiliation history of China and the misfortune of the Chinese nation. Fulfilling national reunification across the Strait, therefore, has always been the unwavering ideal for the mainland's leadership since 1949. When President Xi outlined an explicit blueprint for the "great rejuvenation of the Chinese nation" by 2049 – an updated version of Beijing's national grand strategic goals – many believed Beijing had already set up a definite timetable for resolving the Taiwan issue by reiterating that national reunification "is a necessity of great rejuvenation."[60] Some even argue that this means Beijing will take whatever action deemed necessary, including the use of force, to fulfill reunification before 2049, the timeline for the 100th anniversary of the PRC, suggesting that Beijing may be about to strike up the war drum. Nevertheless, history affords us several lessons that merit attention. In terms of the making of Beijing's Taiwan policy, there has always been a noticeable and consistent guiding principle, that is, that the Taiwan policy must be conducive, instead of detrimental, to the achievement of the national grand strategic goals of the mainland.

After the establishment of the PRC in 1949, Beijing repeatedly stressed that the "most important task" was to "liberate Taiwan and accomplish the cause of unifying China."[61] Yet the outbreak of the Korean War and the military intervention of the US in the Taiwan Strait forced the mainland to indefinitely postpone its amphibious landing operation plan against the KMT administration that had fled to Taiwan. With the signing of the truce agreement on the Korean Peninsula in July 1953, Beijing strategically turned to prioritize nationwide industrialization and socialist transformation, tokened by the introduction of the First Five-Year Plan (1953–1957), in order to rapidly rehabilitate the country's economy, which had been devastated by the decades-long war. Encouraged by the successful initiation of economic reconstruction, Beijing formally proposed its "Four Modernizations" outlook in 1959, aiming to build China into a socialist power with the fulfillment of industrial, agricultural, national defense, and science/technology modernization.[62] From then on, achieving modernization, although periodically deviated by some drastic political developments, like the Cultural Revolution, has become the centerpiece of Beijing's national construction ambition.

Concurrent with the shift of the strategic priority to national development, Beijing transformed its policy of "liberating Taiwan by force" (1949–1955). In May 1955, Premier Zhou Enlai announced during the National People's Congress that the mainland was ready to "liberate Taiwan by peaceful means under possible conditions." It is marked as the first time that Beijing publicly introduced a stance to "liberate Taiwan by peaceful ways."[63] On October 6, 1958, the mainland delivered the "Message to Compatriots in Taiwan from the Defense Ministry of PRC" written by Mao Zedong, in which Beijing proposed to "conduct negotiation" and "achieve peaceful resolution" of the cross-Strait standoff.[64] In accordance with the evolution of mainland China's national strategy and the shift of strategic priority, these statements and proposals represented a significant change in Beijing's Taiwan policy.

The implementation of the economic reform and opening-up strategy of the mainland and the establishment of diplomatic relations between the PRC and the US contributed to an entirely new horizon for the settlement of the Taiwan issue. Since the Third Plenum of the Eleventh Central Committee of the CPC was held in December 1978, Beijing's national strategic priority had been reset. In December 1979, Deng Xiaoping initiated the term "Xiaokang Society," a society of moderate prosperity, as the foremost goal for the PRC's modernization drive, upon which Deng's ambitious outlook was formally expounded as a "three-step development strategy" to achieve basic modernization by the middle of the 21st century.[65] Correspondingly, Beijing started a new round of Taiwan policy adjustments in order to create a favorable cross-Strait situation and international conditions for economic modernization. Deng pushed to formally replace the mainland's use of the term "liberation" (*jiefang*) with "resolution" (*jiejue*) of the Taiwan issue, and formulated the "peaceful reunification strategy."[66] On January 1, 1979, Beijing issued the "Message to Compatriots in Taiwan," which constituted a manifesto of another fundamental policy change of the mainland toward Taiwan. It is the first official mainland document focusing on the Taiwan issue that did not use the phrase "liberating Taiwan." Instead, it proposed, also for the first time, to "put an end to the state of military hostility" through talks between the two sides.[67] On October 1, 1981, Marshal Ye Jianying, then chairman of the NPC, further elaborated on the policy of peaceful reunification in his "Nine-Point Proposal."[68] On June 26, 1983, Deng put forward his well-known "Six-Point Proposal," the cornerstone of the policy of "peaceful reunification and one country two systems," and charted Beijing's Taiwan policy in the "reform and open-up era."[69]

In order to concentrate on economic construction instead of hastily pushing forward reunification, Deng frequently reminded CPC leaders that "it has no bearing on the overall situation if the Taiwan issue would be resolved slower and later."[70] As early as January 16, 1980, when Deng listed three major tasks for mainland China, including opposing hegemony, fulfilling reunification, and modernization development, he emphasized that the "core issue" of the three tasks is modernization.[71] President Jiang Zemin, for the first time, proposed the "three historical missions" in his report to the 16th National Congress of the CPC, among which the first mission was to push forward modernization construction, while "fulfilling national reunification" was listed as the second mission before the third one, "safeguarding world peace and promoting common development."[72] Subsequently, the three historical missions were formally written into the charter of the CPC in October 2007 by President Hu Jintao.

With the achievement of spectacular economic growth since the 1980s, Beijing later updated the roadmap for its national development strategy. In November 2012, President Hu presented a new ambitious blueprint for achieving the "two centennial goals" in 2021 and 2049, respectively.[73] In the report to the 19th National Congress of the CPC in October 2017, President Xi drew up a more concrete two-stage timetable for the two centennial goals and espoused the "Chinese Dream" of national rejuvenation. Under the overarching goal of developing China into a "great modern socialist country," Beijing made clear that the "principal contradiction facing Chinese society" is the "contradiction between unbalanced and inadequate development and the people's ever-growing needs for a better life," a strategic reassessment which would affect the landscape of China's future development. In the report, Xi reiterated the aforementioned three historical missions in the same order and demanded to boost economic development and achieve comprehensive modernization in the lead up to the "great rejuvenation of the Chinese nation."[74] More important, Beijing has a full awareness that the mainland is facing "a new historic juncture in development," and there is still a long way ahead before heralding national rejuvenation, which means that fulfilling the goal of comprehensive modernization still is, and will remain, the top strategic priority for Beijing in the long run.

Looking back into history, for generations of CPC leaders, the accomplishment of reunification has served as subordinate to the fulfillment of the national grand strategy of mainland China, rather than vice versa. In regard to the relationship between modernization and reunification, for example, Deng once explained explicitly that "if we could do a good job of the Four Modernizations, and if our economy could develop well, then our capability to fulfill unification will be different."[75] President Hu also acknowledged the fact that the modernization progress of the mainland would provide "a strong foundation and reliable safeguard" for realizing peaceful reunification.[76] By tracing the Taiwan issue back to the Sino-Japanese War of 1895, President Xi commented that the "Taiwan question originated in a weak and ravaged China, and it will definitely end with China's rejuvenation!"[77] These statements reflect Beijing's keen understanding that building mainland China into a great power based on comprehensive modernization, therefore obtaining an overwhelming advantage over Taiwan, is the necessary precondition to contain Taiwanese independence, deter external interference, and fulfill national reunification.

The same logic also implies the answer to the question of the relationship between reunification and Beijing's current grand strategic goal, namely the "great rejuvenation of the Chinese nation." In other words, should reunification be the cause or the consequence of China's national rejuvenation? Even though achieving reunification across the Taiwan Strait is termed as "an inevitable requirement" (*biran yaoqiu*) for China's national rejuvenation, Beijing clearly understands that reunification should be the consequence, instead of the cause, of its progress in pursuit of the two centennial goals. Beijing endeavors to make the resolution of the Taiwan issue a propellant, rather than a barricade, for the accomplishment of its grand strategy. By and large, it means Beijing prefers to "marginalize" the Taiwan issue rather than "prioritize" it at the top of the strategic agenda before the mainland accomplishes its modernization vision; unless Taipei would pursue a radical de jure Taiwan independence policy that Beijing perceives to be provocative and intolerable.

Prioritization of the modernization momentum explains Beijing's reemphasis of "strategic confidence" and "strategic willpower" (*zhanlve dingli*) in the face of growing domestic appeal to use of force and spiraling US–Taiwan cooperation. In terms of the economic modernization effort, the mainland has become the second-largest economy in the world since 2010, after several decades of rapid development. China's GDP had risen from 66% of the US GDP in 2019 to 71% in 2020, and about 76% by the end of 2021. It is estimated that if the US maintains an average growth rate of 2-3% and China maintains a 5-6% growth rate in the future, China's total economy will catch up with the US by 2028 to 2030. Beijing believes that consistently keeping its economic modernization pace is the best way to steadily close the remaining gap between the US and China, resulting in the dwindling capability of the US to intervene in the Taiwan issue (Figure 4.4 and Table 4.2).

In terms of the military modernization effort, Beijing knows it is still no match for the US on almost every conventional and nuclear measure, and this can discredit its deterrence against Taiwan independence move and the "dual deterrence" imposed by the US. In October 2017, President Xi laid out two PLA modernization goals during his speech to the 19th National Congress of the CPC to "basically complete" PLA modernization by 2035 and to transform the PLA into a "world-class" military by 2049. With the aim of building a force that can ultimately turn the regional military balance around the Taiwan Strait to its advantage and handle the potential worst-case scenario, China is investing heavily in asymmetric equalizers such as long-range anti-ship and hypersonic missiles and developing sophisticated capabilities to conduct joint long-range precision strikes across domains.

In the past decade, the commission of a series of advanced weapon systems, including the J-20, Z-20, and Y-20 aircraft in the Air Force; indigenous aircraft carriers, Type 075 amphibious assault ship, and Type 055 destroyer in the Navy; and DF-26, DF-21D, and DF-17 missiles in the Rocket Force, has contributed to the large-scale expansion of the PLA's arsenal for anti-access/area-denial (A2/AD) combat.[78] For example, the month of November 2021 witnessed the debuts of a two-seat variant of the J-20 stealth fighter, which signified a major boost to the PLA's air combat capabilities, and a carrier-capable naval stealth fighter that would provide the PLA's expanding carrier fleet with a stealthy multirole fighter.[79] Additionally, according to the report disclosed by the Pentagon in November 2021, the PLA is expanding its nuclear arsenal much quicker than predicted and could have 700 deliverable nuclear warheads by 2027 and over 1,000 by 2030, an arsenal two-and-a-half times the size of what the Pentagon anticipated in 2020.[80]

Furthermore, an array of the PLA's futuristic armaments that will operate in space and in the cyber realm is also under fast-track development. For instance, in September 2021, US Air Force Secretary Frank Kendall first suggested that the PLA had conducted a test involving a Fractional

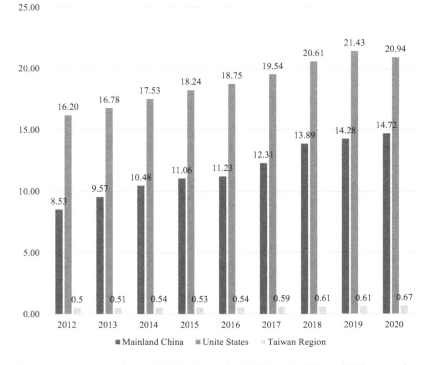

Figure 4.4 A comparison of GDP of mainland China, the US, and Taiwan region (per US$ trillion).

Table 4.2 Comparison of GDP of mainland China, the US, and Taiwan region (per US$ trillion)

	2012	2013	2014	2015	2016	2017	2018	2019	2020
Mainland China	8.53	9.57	10.48	11.06	11.23	12.31	13.89	14.28	14.72
United States	16.20	16.78	17.53	18.24	18.75	19.54	20.61	21.43	20.94
Taiwan region	0.5	0.51	0.54	0.53	0.54	0.59	0.61	0.61	0.67

Sources: The World Bank, GDP (Current US$) – China, United States, 2012–2020, https://data.worldbank.org/indicator/NY.GDP.MKTP.CD?end=2020 &locations=CN-US&start=2012&view=chart; Statistics of Taiwan, GDP of Taiwan, updated to 2021, https://data.worldbank.org/indicator/NY.GDP.MKTP .CD?end=2020&locations=CN-US&start=2012&view=chart.

Orbital Bombardment System (FOBS), a weapon that uses a rocket to boost its payload into low earth orbit, which subsequently deorbits through the atmosphere to its terrestrial target.[81] The rapid pace of China's progress even drove General Mark Milley, the chairman of the Joint Chiefs of Staff, to state that the test of the hypersonic missile was "very close" to the kind of "Sputnik moment."[82] On November 18, 2021, General John Hyten, US vice chairman of the Joint Chiefs of Staff, revealed that Beijing tested a hypersonic missile that "went around the world, dropped off a hypersonic glide vehicle that glided all the way back to China, that impacted a target in China."[83] Just ten days later, Lieutenant General Chance Saltzman, US deputy Space Force chief for operations, confirmed again that PLA's test of a FOBS that deployed a hypersonic glide vehicle was a "very forward-edge technology capability" that Space Force must figure out how to deter as soon as possible.[84] It was also warned by the Pentagon that the accelerating modernization of China's military capabilities through an approach described as "intelligentized" warfare would for sure provide Beijing "with more credible military options in a Taiwan contingency."[85] Undoubtedly, the ever-growing development of the PLA's capability in both quality and quantity will gradually turn the military balance in the Taiwan Strait to mainland China's advantage (Figure 4.5 and Table 4.3).

Conclusion

Since the DPP's election victory in 2016, the cross-Strait relationship has entered uncharted waters and tension has gradually risen.[86] This chapter argues that Beijing, being more confident in its capability to contain Taiwan's de jure independence venture due to its expanding power advantage, has shifted to target the ever-growing momentum of perpetuating de facto independence, now seen as the foremost concern. After several decades of wrestling with the mainland, the Taiwanese have also realized that the unrealistic pursuit of de jure independence would derail cross-Strait peace and stability, risking a disastrous conflict. To indefinitely maintain the de facto independence of Taiwan, "permanent peaceful separation," has become the most favorable choice for both KMT and DPP politicians, as well as for most of the Taiwanese population, who refuse to accept reunification. This reality has transformed the threat perception of Beijing, which neither wants to take any chance to allow Taiwan to achieve de jure independence nor tolerate the cross-Strait separation lasting forever. How to prevent the de facto independence of Taiwan from perpetuating – particularly by ensuring all-round preparedness and substantially promoting pro-unification dynamics among the Taiwanese – has become the most significant challenge for Beijing.

In order to achieve national reunification, Beijing tried to encourage the Chiang Kai-shek and Chiang Ching-kuo administrations to conduct political negotiations and reach mutually accepted resolutions. However, this "placing hope on the Taiwanese administration" guideline was impeded when Taiwan transformed into a two-party democracy in the 1990s. Irritated by the pro-independence direction of the Lee and Chen administrations, Beijing switched to place the hope of reunification more on the Taiwanese people through economic integration and social engagement. However, rising anti-China sentiment, exemplified by the 2014 Sunflower Movement and the emphatic victories of the DPP in the 2016 and 2020 presidential elections, has driven Beijing to "place more hope on the mainland itself" in practice, while politically still claiming to "place hope on the Taiwanese." Through the new guideline based on self-reliance, Beijing will be focused on its own strategic agenda and preferences, while taking the initiative to lead and dominate the future evolution of cross-Strait relations.

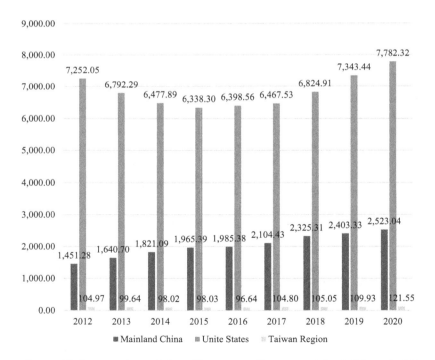

Figure 4.5 A comparison of the military expenditure of mainland China, the US, and Taiwan region (per US$100 million).

Table 4.3 Comparison of the military expenditure of mainland China, the US, and Taiwan region (per US$100 million)

	2012	2013	2014	2015	2016	2017	2018	2019	2020
Mainland China	1451.28	1640.70	1821.09	1965.39	1985.38	2 104,43	2325.31	2403.33	2523.04
United States	7252.05	6792.29	6477.89	6338.30	6398.56	6 467.53	6824.91	7343.44	7782.32
Taiwan region	104.97	99.64	98.02	98.03	96.64	104,80	105.05	109.93	121.55

Source: SIPRI Military Expenditure Database, 1988–2020, https://sipri.org/sites/default/files/Data%20for%20all%20countries%201988%E2%80%932020%20in%20constant%20%282019%29%20USD%20%28pdf%29.pdf.

As Beijing has reiterated that it "preserves the option of taking all necessary measures" to fulfill reunification, which is the "inevitable requirement" of its national rejuvenation ambition by 2049, many wonder whether Beijing has forged a definite timetable and will resort to the use of force to meet its timeline, thus making the Taiwan issue center stage again and representing a major military flashpoint in the Asia-Pacific. However, by examining the evolution of Beijing's Taiwan strategy, this chapter suggests that the relevant policies are always formulated in accordance with the strategic priority of the mainland in handling multiple internal and external challenges. For Beijing, given reunification is an "inevitable option" independent of Taipei's intention and practice, rather than setting up a rigid timetable to tie its own hands, more important is when and how the fulfillment of reunification will be most beneficial to the mainland's overall national strategy. Therefore, even though Beijing is frustrated by Tsai's refusal to embrace the one-China principle leading to the face-off across the Strait, Beijing will continue to prioritize the achievement of its national grand strategic goal, specifically the fulfillment of comprehensive modernization, rather than resolve the Taiwan issue by force shortly, unless the Taiwan administration pursues a radical de jure independence policy that is intolerable to Beijing in the near future.

Notes

1 Lin Gang, "Beijing's New Strategies Towards a Changing Taiwan," *Journal of Contemporary China* 25, no. 99 (January 2016), 321–335.
2 Wang Zhenwei, "Norm Regress: A Discussion on the Current Situation of the Cross-Strait Relations," *Taiwan Research Journal*, no. 5 (2021), 17–25. For example, the Shanghai Academy of Social Sciences and the *Global Times*, one of the most popular newspapers in mainland China, jointly launched an online survey about the Taiwan issue in April 2016 before the inauguration of Tsai. The poll, even though it was an informal online poll far from precision and rigorousness, showed 85% of the netizen supported to "fulfill reunification by force." To a large extent, it reflected the frustration of the mainland public opinion about the DPP's victory in the 2016 election and the pessimism for the peace and development prospect across the Strait.
3 Xi Jinping, "The Speech on the 40th Anniversary of the Issuance of 'Message to Compatriots in Taiwan,'" Xinhua News Agency, January 2, 2019, http://www.xinhuanet.com/tw/2019-01/02/c_1210028622.htm; "Xi Jinping: Remarks on the 110th Anniversary of the Revolution of 1911," Xinhua News Agency, October 9, 2021, http://www.news.cn/politics/leaders/2021-10/09/c_1127941568.htm.
4 Brad Lendon, "Chinese Threat to Taiwan 'Closer to Us Than Most Think,' Top US Admiral Says," CNN, March 24, 2021, https://www.cnn.com/2021/03/24/asia/indo-pacific-commander-aquilino-hearing-taiwan-intl-hnk-ml/index.html.
5 Sandra Oudkirk, "Remarks by AIT Director Sandra Oudkirk at the Press Conference Opening," American Institute in Taiwan, October 29, 2021, https://

www.ait.org.tw/remarks-by-ait-director-sandra-oudkirk-at-the-press-confer-ence-opening.

6 Ben Blanchard, "Taiwan Won't Start a War with China But Will Defend Itself 'Full On,' Say Defense Minister," Reuters, October 14, 2021, https://www.reu-ters.com/world/china/taiwan-defence-minister-says-china-will-have-ability-mount-full-scale-invasion-2021-10-06.

7 Will Ripley and Eric Cheung, "Taiwan's President Says the Threat from China Is Increasing 'Every Day' and Confirms Presence of US Military Trainers on the Island," CNN, October 28, 2021, https://www.cnn.com/2021/10/27/asia/tsai-ingwen-taiwan-china-interview-intl-hnk/index.html.

8 Opinion polls made by the Mainland Affairs Council of Taiwan and Election Study Center of the National Chengchi University (NCCU). See "Changes in the Unification–Independence Stances of Taiwanese as Tracked by Election Studies Center, NCCU (1994–2021.06)," NCCU, June 2021, https://esc.nccu.edu.tw/PageDoc/Detail?fid=7805&id=6962.

9 Hsiao-kuang Shih and Dennis Xie, "KMT Task Force Unveils Four Pillars for Stable, Peaceful Cross-Strait Relations," *Taipei Times*, June 20, 2020, https://www.taipeitimes.com/News/front/archives/2020/06/20/2003738531.

10 Chen Yun, "KMT's Lin Wei-chou Moots Axing 'Zhongguo,'" *Taipei Times*, October 11, 2020, https://www.taipeitimes.com/News/front/archives/2020/10/11/2003744972.

11 "Xi Congratulates Eric Chu on Election as KMT Chief," Xinhua News Agency, September 27, 2021, http://english.scio.gov.cn/m/topnews/2021-09/27/content_77777138.htm.

12 Matthew Strong, "Taiwan Poll Finds 85% Support Status Quo," *Taiwan News*, November 19, 2021, https://www.taiwannews.com.tw/en/news/4350512.

13 Sun Yafu, "Development of Cross-Strait Relations (1987–2012)," *Journal of Political Science*, no. 4 (2015), 3–18.

14 Huang Jiashu, "An Analysis of the Cross-Strait Political Relations and Tsai Ing-wen's 'Maintaining the Status Quo,'" *Taiwan Studies*, no. 5 (2015), 1–6.

15 Amber Wang, "Taiwan 'Already Independent', Tsai Warns China," AFP (access from Yahoo News), January 15, 2020, https://news.yahoo.com/taiwan-already-independent-tsai-warns-china-062513557.html.

16 Wang Weinan and Zhang Xianhua, "Theoretical Reflections on the Cross-Strait Relations since 1949," *Taiwan Studies*, no. 6 (2017), 8–15.

17 Chen Kongli, "Five Stages in the Process of Mutual Recognition between the Two Sides," *Taiwan Research Journal*, no. 6 (2017), 1–6.

18 Xi Jinping, "The Speech on the 40th Anniversary."

19 Xi Jinping, "Report at the Nineteenth National Congress of the CPC," *People's Daily*, October 28, 2017, http://cpc.people.com.cn/n1/2017/1028/c64094-29613660.html.

20 Thomas J. Christensen, "The Contemporary Security Dilemma: Deterring a Taiwan Conflict," *The Washington Quarterly* 25, no. 4 (Autumn 2002), 5–21; Richard Bush, *Untying the Knot: Making Peace in the Taiwan Strait* (Washington DC: Brookings Institution Press, 2015).

21 Zuo Xiying, "Unbalanced Deterrence: Coercive Threat, Reassurance and the US-China Rivalry in Taiwan Strait," *The Pacific Review* 34, no. 2 (December 2019), 1–30.

22 Richard C. Bush, "The Trump Administration's Chaotic Taiwan Policy," The Brookings Institution, May 16, 2018, https://www.brookings.edu/wp-content

/uploads/2018/05/Bush_The-Trump-administration's-chaotic-Taiwan-policy
.pdf.
23 The full name of the TAIPEI Act is Taiwan Allies International Protection and
Enhancement Initiative Act.
24 Xin Qiang, "The Resurgence of the Pro-Taiwan Force in the US Congress and
Its Impact," *Contemporary International Relations*, no. 7 (2019), 1–9.
25 "White House Backtracks after Biden Appears to Say US Would Defend Taiwan
against China," *Guardian*, August 19, 2021, https://www.theguardian.com/
world/2021/aug/20/biden-taiwan-china-us-defence.
26 Yang Zhaoyan, "Refuting U.S. Unreliability, Biden States: If Taiwan Is Invaded,
U.S. Will Respond," CNA, August 20, 2021, https://www.cna.com.tw/news/
firstnews/202108200003.aspx.
27 Kevin Liptak, "Biden Vows to Protect Taiwan in Event of Chinese Attack,"
CNN, October 22, 2021, https://www.cnn.com/2021/10/21/politics/taiwan
-china-biden-town-hall/index.html.
28 Laura Kelly, "White House Says No Change in US Policy toward Taiwan," *The
Hill*, October 22, 2021, https://thehill.com/policy/international/578001-white
-house-says-no-change-in-us-policy-toward-taiwan.
29 Antony Blinken, "Supporting Taiwan's Participation in the UN System," U.S.
Department of State, October 26, 2021, https://www.state.gov/supporting-tai-
wans-participation-in-the-un-system.
30 "Ministry of Foreign Affairs Stresses Four Basic Facts on U.S. Secretary of
State's Remarks on Taiwan," Xinhua News Agency, October 28, 2021, http://
www.gwytb.gov.cn/bmst/202110/t20211028_12387360.htm.
31 ROC Central News Agency, "Taiwan President Tsai Ing-wen's National Day
Speech (Full Text)," *Taiwan Times*, October 10, 2021, https://www.taiwannews
.com.tw/en/news/4311090.
32 Taiwan Affairs Office of the State Council of PRC, "White Paper: The One-
China Principle and the Taiwan Issue," February 21, 2000, http://www.gwytb
.gov.cn/zt/zylszl/baipishu/201101/t20110118_1700148.htm.
33 Xi Jinping, "Xi Jinping's Speech at the Meeting to Commemorate the 150th
Anniversary of Sun Yat-sen's Birth," Xinhua News Agency, November 12,
2016, http://www.xinhuanet.com//politics/2016-11/11/c_1119897047.htm.
34 "China's Top Legislator Stresses Resolutely Opposing 'Taiwan Independence,'"
Xinhua News Agency, May 29, 2020, http://www.xinhuanet.com/english/2020
-05/29/c_139098708.htm.
35 "President Xi Jinping Had a Virtual Meeting with US President Joe Biden,"
Ministry of Foreign Affairs of PRC, November 16, 2021, https://www.fmprc
.gov.cn/mfa_eng/zxxx_662805/202111/t20211116_10448843.html.
36 Huang Jiashu, "On the Path Transformation of Peaceful Reunification," *Taiwan
Studies*, no. 6 (2017), 1–7.
37 Taiwan Affairs Office of the State Council of PRC, *China's Taiwan Issue*
(Beijing: Jiuzhou Press, 2015).
38 Mao Zedong, *Manuscripts of Mao Zedong since the Establishment of the
People's Republic of China*, Vol. 7 (Beijing: Central Party Literature Press,
1987), 457–461.
39 Henry Kissinger, *On China* (New York: Penguin Press, 2011), 280.
40 Ye Jianying, "Principle and Policy about Taiwan's Return to Motherland and
Fulfillment of Peaceful Reunification," *People's Daily*, October 1, 1981, http://
tga.mofcom.gov.cn/article/ls/jingmaofagui/200712/20071205294687.shtml.

41 Deng Xiaoping, *Selected Works of Deng Xiaoping*, Vol. 3 (Beijing: Renmin Press, 1993).

42 Shao Zonghai, *Cross-Straits Political Relations under the New Situation* (Taipei: Wu-Nan Book Inc., 2011), 164.

43 Su Chi, *Twenty Years of Turbulent Cross-Strait Relations: A Chronology* (Taipei: Common Wealth Culture, 2014).

44 Lin Jin, "The Pattern of 'Taiwan Independence Movement' after Taiwan Political Transformation," *Taiwan Studies*, no. 2 (2018), 1–7.

45 Nancy Bernkopf Tucker, *Dangerous Strait: The U.S.–Taiwan–China Crisis* (New York: Columbia University Press, 2005).

46 Jiang Zemin, "Keep Fighting for the Accomplishment of National Reunification Cause," Xinhua News Agency, January 30, 1995, http://www.scio.gov.cn/wszt/wz/Document/854015/854015.htm.

47 "March 4, 2005: President Hu Jintao Sets Forth Guidelines on Taiwan," *China Daily*, March 4, 2005, https://www.chinadaily.com.cn/china/19thcpcnational congress/2013-03/01/content_29715055.htm.

48 Xi Jinping, "The Speech on the 40th Anniversary."

49 The Standing Committee of the Fifth National People's Congress, "Message to Compatriots in Taiwan," January 1, 1979, https://language.chinadaily.com.cn/a/201901/02/WS5c2c55eea310d91214052164.html.

50 Sun Yafu and Li Peng, *40 Years of Cross-Straits Relations (1979–2019)* (Beijing: Jiuzhou Press, 2020), 168.

51 Xin Qiang, "Beyond Power Politics: Institutions Building and Mainland China's Taiwan Policy Transition," *Journal of Contemporary China* 19, no. 65 (2010), 525–539.

52 Chen Fang-Yu, Yen Wei-ting, Wang Austin Horng-en, and Hioe Brian, "The Taiwanese See Themselves As Taiwanese, Not As Chinese," *Washington Post*, January 2, 2017, https://www.washingtonpost.com/news/monkey-cage/wp/2017/01/02/yes-taiwan-wants-one-china-but-which-china-does-it-want.

53 Zhong Yang, "Explaining National Identity Shift in Taiwan," *Journal of Contemporary China* 25, no. 99 (2016), 336–352.

54 Opinion polls made by the Mainland Affairs Council of Taiwan and Election Study Center of the National Chengchi University

55 "Xi Jinping Emphasize: Stick to the Path of Cross-Strait Peaceful Development and Advocate Mutual Development to Benefit the People across the Strait," Xinhua News Agency, March 4, 2015, http://www.xinhuanet.com//politics/2015-03/04/c_1114523789.htm.

56 "Director Liu Jieyi's Speech at the Symposium on the 5th Anniversary of the Historic Cross-Strait Leaders' Meeting," Association for Relations Across the Taiwan Strait, November 6, 2020, http://www.arats.com.cn/yw/202011/t20201107_12305385.htm.

57 "Full Text: Communique of 6th Plenary Session of 19th CPC Central Committee," The National People's Congress of the PRC, November 12, 2021, http://www.npc.gov.cn/englishnpc/c23934/202111/c91cf9aa6aee453b8ce8160b00cc8ba8.shtml.

58 The previous two resolutions were issued under former leaders Mao Zedong in 1945 and Deng Xiaoping in 1981. See "Full Text: Resolution of the CPC Central Committee on the Major Achievements and Historical Experience of the Party over the Past Century," Xinhua News Agency, November 16, 2021, http://www.news.cn/english/2021-11/16/c_1310314611.htm.

59 Xi Jinping, "The Speech on the 40th Anniversary."
60 Xi Jinping, "Report at the Nineteenth National Congress of the CPC."
61 Taiwan Affairs Office of the State Council of PRC, *China's Taiwan Issue*.
62 Mao Zedong, *Collected Works of Mao Zedong*, Vol. 7 (Beijing: Renmin Press, 1999), 116.
63 Taiwan Affairs Office of the State Council of PRC, *China's Taiwan Issue*, 30.
64 Zedong, *Collected Works of Mao Zedong*, 420–422.
65 Deng Xiaoping, *Selected Works of Deng Xiaoping*, Vol. 3, 226.
66 Deng Xiaoping, *Chronicle of Deng Xiaoping's Thought 1975–1997* (Beijing: Central Party Literature Press, 1998), 53.
67 The Standing Committee of the Fifth National People's Congress, "Message to Compatriots in Taiwan."
68 Ye Jianying, "Doctrine and Policy Concerning Taiwan's Return to the Motherland and Fulfill Peaceful Reunification," *People's Daily*, October 1, 1981.
69 Deng Xiaoping, *Selected Works of Deng Xiaoping*, Vol. 3, 30–31.
70 Deng Xiaoping, *Selected Works of Deng Xiaoping*, Vol. 3, 84–87.
71 Deng Xiaoping, *Selected Works of Deng Xiaoping*, Vol. 2 (Beijing: Renmin Press, 1989), 239–241.
72 Jiang Zemin, "Full Text of Jiang Zemin's Report at 16th Party Congress," Xinhua News Agency, 8 November, https://www.mfa.gov.cn/chn//pds/ziliao/zyjh/t10855.htm.
73 The first and short-term goal for Beijing is completing the process of building a moderately well-off society and accelerating the modernization process by the time the CPC would celebrate its centenary in 2021. The second and mid-term goal is to build China into a modern country and reach the level of moderately developed countries by the time the PRC would celebrate its centenary in 2049.
74 Xi Jinping, "Report at the Nineteenth National Congress of the CPC."
75 Deng Xiaoping, *Selected Works of Deng Xiaoping*, Vol. 2, 239–241.
76 Hu Jintao, "Addresses Commemorating the 30th Anniversary of the Issuance of Message to Compatriots in Taiwan," Xinhua News Agency, December 31, 2008, http://www.gov.cn/ldhd/2008-12/31/content_1193074.htm.
77 Xi Jinping, "The Speech on the 40th Anniversary."
78 Xin Qiang, "Strategic High-Risk Assets: Power Structure, Sino-US Relations and the Evolution of Taiwan's Strategic Role," *Taiwan Research Journal*, no. 4 (2020), 72–83.
79 Tyler Rogoway, "This Is Our First Look at a Two-Seat Variant of China's J-20 Stealth Fighter (Updated)," October 26, 2021, The War Zone, https://www.thedrive.com/the-war-zone/42892/is-this-our-first-look-at-a-two-seat-variant-of-chinas-j-20-stealth-fighter; Tyler Rogoway, "China's New Carrier-Capable Stealth Fighter's Canopy Is Its Most Intriguing Feature," December 1, 2021, The War Zone, https://www.thedrive.com/the-war-zone/43323/chinas-new-carrier-capable-stealth-fighters-canopy-is-its-most-intriguing-feature.
80 US Department of Defense, "Military and Security Developments Involving the People's Republic of China 2021," November 2021, https://media.defense.gov/2021/Nov/03/2002885874/-1/-1/0/2021-CMPR-FINAL.PDF.
81 Colin Clark and Theresa Hitchens, "'Global Strike From Space;' Did Kendall Reveal Chinese Threat?" Breaking Defense, September 29, 2021, https://breakingdefense.com/2021/09/global-strike-from-space-did-kendall-reveal-chinese-threat/.

82 "China's Hypersonic Missile Test 'close to Sputnik moment', Says US General," *Guardian*, October 28, 2021.

83 Chandelis Duster, "Top Military Leader Says China's Hypersonic Missile Test 'Went around the World,'" CNN, November 18, 2021, https://www.cnn.com /2021/11/17/politics/john-hyten-china-hypersonic-weapons-test/index.html.

84 "It Is a FOBS, Space Force's Saltzman Confirms Amid Chinese Weapon Test Confusion," *Breaking Defense*, November 29, 2021, https://breakingdefense .com/2021/11/its-a-fobs-space-forces-saltzman-confirms-amid-chinese-weap-ons-test-confusion.

85 US Department of Defense, "Military and Security Developments Involving the People's Republic of China 2021."

86 David Brown, "A Fraught Cross-Strait Relationship," National Committee on American Foreign Policy Report, October 2018, pp. 90–99.

5 Conclusion

Navigating the cross-Strait turbulence

There is little doubt that the current cross-Taiwan Strait situation, fraught with peril and tension, is being navigated into even more turbulent waters. While the cross-Strait tension is growing within the context of an intensifying China–US strategic rivalry, the Taiwan issue is widely cautioned as the most likely, if not the only, powder keg in East Asia that might drag China and the US into a military standoff.

Broadly, it has not been unusual for the world to observe some level of tension across the Strait in the past seven decades. However, what deserves a more comprehensive and in-depth reflection and examination is understanding why and how cross-Strait relationships were forced to undergo such a stark transition from peaceful development to spiraling confrontation in a few short years. During Ma Ying-jeou's administration from 2008 to 2016, Beijing and Taipei had jointly pursued cooperative and constructive policies based on the 1992 Consensus. Consequently, mainland China formulated its institutionalism-oriented strategy toward Taiwan in line with the neo-functionalism derived from European experiences, assuming that economic cooperation, education exchange, and society interaction will bridge the divide between the two sides, eventually leading to social accommodation, political integration, and national reunification. After an eight-year period of cross-Strait animosity during Chen Shui-bian's administration, the peaceful development of cross-Strait relations made the world breathe a sigh of relief.

Nonetheless, observers across the globe had to hold their breath once again since Tsai Ing-wen took power in 2016. Beijing's optimistic expectation for a new era of "cross-Strait peaceful development" foundered on the stunning fiascos of the Kuomintang (KMT) in both 2016 and 2020 presidential elections, despite the visible success of the cross-Strait détente under Ma reflected in deescalating tensions, an improvement in Taiwan's international space, and accelerating economic and social exchanges across the Strait. The Tsai administration, encouraged by consecutive landslide presidential

DOI: 10.4324/9781003163275-5

campaign victories, has made clear that it resolved to refute the one-China principle and intended to distance Taipei from Beijing's political embrace and economic orbit in order to maintain Taiwan's de facto independence or fulfill de jure independence if possible. Frustrated by the deteriorating cross-Strait relationship and irritated by Taipei's steadfast abnegation of the one-China principle, Beijing reshaped its Taiwan policy framework in regard to the new political developments in Taiwan and began to pursue a set of much more confrontational measures to deter Taipei from moving toward independence, while still trying to maintain the vibrant economic and trade exchanges across the Strait.

To date, Beijing has established two sets of interchangeable policy frameworks in the face of the normality of power transition on the island. When the island is ruled by a party accepting of the one-China principle, be it the KMT, the Democratic Progress Party (DPP), or some other political party, Beijing will pursue peaceful development and advocate comprehensive rapprochement across the Strait. On the contrary, when the island is ruled by a party that rejects the one-China principle, Beijing will readily switch to the dual-track "selective engagement" framework. In the foreseeable future, peaceful development and selective engagement will be the two regular and routine policy alternatives, hinging on the ruling party's stance on the one-China principle.

For Beijing, the best scenario is that the KMT will continue to advocate the 1992 Consensus and endorse the one-China principle, while the DPP will adjust its traditional refutation and creatively find a similar term like the "1992 Consensus" that can be simultaneously welcomed and accepted by the two sides across the Strait, so as to resolve the stalemate between Beijing and the DPP once and for all and defuse the potentially precarious situation. As was reiterated by President Hu and reaffirmed by President Xi, "No matter who he is and which political party it is, and no matter what they said and did in the past, we're willing to talk with them" as long as they recognize the one-China principle.[1] The worst scenario is that the two major parties on the island will reject the one-China principle driven by the anti-China populist emotion and move together to pursue de jure Taiwan independence or maintain de facto Taiwan independence forever. It will push Beijing to the corner and lead to the abandonment of its decade-long peaceful reunification doctrine.

Currently, the political positions of Beijing and Tsai's administration about whether the two sides across the Taiwan Strait belong to "one China" still run in parallel. It is unlikely that the two sides will change their uncompromising stances, which means there is little room for improvement in the cross-Strait relationship in the near future. The enduring frostiness and, at times, open hostility between the two sides might nudge the tense cross-Strait relationship, as some analysts warned, to the edge of a security crisis. Even worse, such a cross-Strait crisis, given the potential military intervention of the US, implies a much graver risk of a full-scale conflict between China and the US.

As a result, Taipei sought to increase its military budget for more advanced weapons from the US in order to pursue asymmetrical capabilities that could turn Taiwan into a "fortress," a "hedgehog," a "porcupine," or a "poison frog," and even buying smaller, mobile weapons systems to mount a "guerrilla-style defense."[2] In the meantime, Washington has repeatedly expressed concern over the break out of a cross-Strait conflict, sending numerous signals to Beijing that the support of the US to Taiwan is "rock solid." The "invasion panic" in Washington and Taipei, or the anxiety about the impending mainland attack on Taiwan, drove Washington to modify its one-China policy by incrementally strengthening US–Taiwan interactions.[3] Some defense and political analysts also strongly encouraged the US government to change its long-standing policy of "strategic ambiguity" into "strategic clarity" in order to "keep the peace" and "make clear to China that force will not stand" by making explicit that the US "would respond to any Chinese use of force against Taiwan."[4]

Nonetheless, from the perspective of mainland China, the aforementioned argument reflects a widespread but misleading myth that it is the "security commitment" of the US to Taiwan, either as clear as the Mutual Defense Treaty or as opaque as the strategic ambiguity policy, that has successfully deterred Beijing from launching a reunification war and safeguarded the peace and stability across the Strait in the past decades. Fair to say, it is one of the contributing reasons, however by no means the vital and fundamental one. After all, neither the signing of the Mutual Defense Treaty had deterred the PLA from bombarding Kinmen Island in 1958, nor did the "dual deterrence" derived from the strategic ambiguity policy of the US prevent the 1995–1996 Taiwan Strait Crisis from happening. Undoubtedly, the mainland has long had the ability to undertake military actions, at least to capture Taiwan's closest offshore islands including Kinmen and Matsu, which lie only 10 kilometers off Fujian's coast but has restrained itself from doing so for decades. As a report delivered in October 2021 by the Center for a New American Security stated, the US has "few credible options" to respond if the mainland were to seize a set of islands under the control of Taiwan in the South China Sea.[5] A *National Interest* article titled "Could the US Lose a War with China Over Taiwan?" also doubted the possibility of Washington winning in the Taiwan Strait if a war breaks out there.[6] As warned by some US senior generals, it is even not wild to imagine that the American military might lose a potential conflict over Taiwan "before it started."[7]

Even though the risk of US involvement will definitely complicate Beijing's calculation of costs and benefits and make a use-of-force decision a difficult one,[8] the foremost reason for the maintenance of "no use of force" across the narrow strait actually lies in the consistent belief held by successive generations of Beijing's leadership that fulfilling peaceful reunification based on the one-China principle "best serves the fundamental interests of the Chinese nation, including the Taiwan compatriots," whereby the mainland "must do its utmost with utmost sincerity to strive for peaceful reunification."[9] On May 29, 2020, Li Zhanshu, chairman of the National People's Congress (NPC), proclaimed, "Wherever there is a glimmer of a peaceful solution, we will work a hundred times harder for it."[10] The pledge was echoed most recently by President Xi in his virtual meeting with President Biden on November 16, 2021, by stressing that Beijing "will strive for the prospect of peaceful reunification with utmost sincerity and efforts."[11] Indeed, it is Beijing's "commitment to pursuing peace and prosperity across the Taiwan Strait" that has long prevented a potential military conflict over the island.[12]

Beijing's peaceful reunification commitment and strategic patience, of course, are not groundless, but fundamentally hinged on two vital preconditions. The first is the establishment of and commitment to the one-China policy, as well as the political stance of "not supporting Taiwan independence" adopted by the US since 1972, even though Beijing is unhappy about the passage of the Taiwan Relations Act and continuous arms sales to Taiwan. For example, the decision of Clinton's administration to invite Lee Teng-hui to visit the US in 1995, regarded by Beijing as a blatant provocation of the one-China principle, was responded to by missile launch tests and large-scale military maneuvers by the People's Liberation Army (PLA). On the other hand, it was the strong and explicit opposition of the Bush administration to Chen Shui-bian's pro-independence activities from 2002 to 2008, including the infamous failure of the referendum on seeking membership in the UN under the name Taiwan, that reassured Beijing and consolidated the strategic mutual trust, reducing the cross-Strait tensions and stabilizing the East Asia region.[13] To a large extent, the policy of dual deterrence of the US did play an important and constructive role in maintaining the cross-Strait situation of no use of force mainly because it helped to deter Taipei from overtly pursuing independence-focused policies, which is always the bottom-line precipitating the use of force by Beijing, rather than actually deterring Beijing from using force, particularly when the military superiority of the US is dwindling. Provided that Taiwan announces de jure independence or "the separatist forces for 'Taiwan independence' provoke us [the mainland]," as Xi warned, nothing can stop Beijing from abandoning the principle of peaceful unification and resorting to force.[14]

The second precondition is the acceptance of and compliance with the one-China principle, no matter willingly or reluctantly, of the Taiwan administration, even though this principle has been eroded by the KMT. For Beijing, as long as Taipei accepts the one-China principle, the people on the two sides are "part of the same Chinese family," or as President Xi commented at the Xi–Ma meeting, "We are brothers connected by flesh even if our bones are broken, we are a family whose blood is thicker than water."[15] The appeal of Chairman Mao that "Chinese shall not fight Chinese" explained the "even-day ceasefire," one of the most dramatic and interesting events in human military history. The on-again, off-again shelling of Kinmen "only in odd-numbered days" by the PLA lasted from October 1958 to January 1979 when Taiwan was ruled by KMT's Chiang Kai-shek and Chiang Ching-kuo, lifelong sworn foes of the Communist Party of China (CPC). In light of the consensus reached between Beijing and Taipei centering on the one-China principle in 1992, the two sides held the historic Wang–Koo meeting in April 1993, which was heralded as a huge step forward for cross-Strait peace and stability.

Unfortunately, two significant destabilizing dynamics are imposing unprecedented challenges to Beijing's confidence in fulfilling peaceful reunification. First is Taiwan's deviation from the one-China principle. The one-China principle insisted by Beijing is in sharp contrast with the "One Side, One State" position embraced by the DPP. It is hard to imagine that the DPP will shift its ground after successive campaign victories. Additionally, the KMT has begun to half-heartedly deviate from its prior position on the 1992 Consensus and intended to transform itself into a complete "indigenized," namely a "Taiwan-centric," party in order to prevail over the DPP. Aside from some policy differences between the KMT and the DPP, Beijing will be confronted by two essentially "no-unification parities" on the island in the long run. What's more, the development of Taiwanese identity is increasingly turning away from Chinese identity and the recognition that "the two sides belong to one China," hence, leading to the resolute opposition to reunification across the Strait in any form, by any means, and under any timeline.

For Beijing, as reunification is termed as an "inevitable requirement" for achieving the "China Dream" and realizing the "great rejuvenation of the Chinese nation," it will face more and more domestic pressure to fulfill national reunification and become less tolerant to current "peaceful separation" between the two sides. As the power balance across the Strait continues to swing decisively in Beijing's favor, coupled with the growing aspiration of Taipei to sustain "permanent peaceful separation," Beijing is likely to review the feasibility and efficiency of its Taiwan policy and further shift its focus in the future to press Taipei to start the political negotiation leading to final reunification, so as to extinguish Taipei's hope for "no-unification forever."

Second is the US backpedaling of its one-China policy. For Beijing, the US one-China policy, the political foundation, and the litmus test of China–US relations have been severely eroded by successive US governments. Particularly, the provocative manipulation of the Taiwan issue by the Trump administration, including the Trump–Tsai phone call in December 2016, the statement by State Secretary Mike Pompeo that "Taiwan is not a part of China" in November 2020, the lifting of limitations on the US–Taiwan official interactions in January 2021, adding the "Six Assurances" to its one-China policy framework, as well as the signatures of a series of acts aiming to "normalize" US–Taiwan political and military relationship, confirmed Beijing's belief that Washington is determined to incrementally cast away its decades-long one-China policy in order to strategically compete with China.[16]

The Biden presidency somewhat rekindled within Beijing the hope that it might bring US cross-Strait policymaking back to normalcy and rationality, even though Beijing clearly knows that "prevailing in strategic competition with China" and "supporting Taiwan, a leading democracy and a critical economic and security partner, in line with longstanding American commitments" will remain one of the top foreign policy priorities of the Biden administration.[17] Even though President Biden, a seasoned politician who has much better knowledge of the Taiwan issue than his predecessor, has stated that the US "is not encouraging independence" of Taiwan and will stick to the one-China policy, Beijing has paid more attention to the behaviors than the rhetoric of Washington. Nonetheless, an array of eye-poking behaviors, such as officially allowing for the first time Taipei's representative to Washington to participate at Biden's inauguration ceremony, sending its ambassador to Palau to visit Taiwan, the "misspeaking" of President Biden at least two times in August and October 2021 that the US would protect Taiwan should the mainland launch an attack, inviting Taiwan to the Summit for Democracy as if it were a nation, referring to Taiwan as a "country" by State Secretary Antony Blinken in March 2021, the landing of senior US officials on Taiwanese soil in military planes, making public the deployment of US special troops on Taiwan, holding the official US–Taiwan Economic Prosperity Partnership Dialogue, the consecutive sailing of US warships through the Taiwan Strait, challenging UN Resolution 2758, and claiming to assist Taiwan's future participation throughout the United Nations system in October 2021, made Beijing believe that Washington is intending to "play the Taiwan card" to the furthest extent in order to outcompete China.

For Beijing, the Biden administration, incentivized by a domestic bipartisan "China-bashing" mentality, is just paying lip service to the one-China policy and endeavoring to gradually turn the policy into simply an empty and meaningless concept. Step by step, the "informal" and "unofficial" US–Taiwan relationship as the China–US Three Communiques defined, will be twisted into an "informal official relationship" or a "formal unofficial relationship." That was why China's Foreign Minister Wang Yi requested Secretary Blinken on October 31, 2021, to "pursue a real One China policy, not a fake One China policy," and "fulfill its commitments to China, rather than betray its promises."[18] In his virtual meeting with President Biden, Xi addressed without equivocation the "repeated attempts by the Taiwan authorities to look for US support for their independence agenda" as well as "the intention of some Americans to use Taiwan to contain China," and warned that such moves are as dangerous as "playing with fire."[19] Obviously, the US backpedaling on its one-China policy will rock or even wipe out the fragile mutual trust between Beijing and Washington, and force Beijing to further adjust its Taiwan policy in a more confrontational manner.

The cross-Strait relationship has stumbled into its worst state since 1996 and been thrust into much uncertainty again after a period of peaceful development. China–US relations have also slumped to the lowest point since 1972 because of the combative security, economic, and diplomatic policies of the Trump administration. Meanwhile, US–Taiwan relations have hit an all-time high since 1979. The dangerous dynamics inherent in this unbalanced trilateral interaction, basically unchanged after President Biden assumed office, has driven the cross-Strait situation into turbulent waters, characterized by intensifying tension and rivalry.[20]

There is no doubt that maintaining cross-Strait peace and stability is in the interest of all three parties. Amidst the gridlocked rivalry across the Taiwan Strait and the Pacific, it is imperative for policymakers to think over how to rescue the trilateral relations from a downward spiral and establish a positive-sum cycle conducive to collaboration and cooperation. Although setting up positive-sum dynamics among the three parties is hard, it is not impossible if some necessary and sufficient conditions could be temporarily met. In the history of cross-Strait relations, the period closest to a positive-sum situation was the eight-year presidency of the Ma administration, from which we can infer the conditions for the realization of positive-sum dynamics.

First and foremost, the two sides across the Strait reached a consensus, albeit with ambiguity and subtle disagreement, on the one-China principle. On the one hand, Taipei cast away Chen Shui-bian's confrontational policy and promised not to pursue a Taiwan independence agenda to provoke Beijing. On the other hand, Beijing refrained from taking military measures to deter Taipei's pro-independence momentum and turned to promote reunification through the path of peaceful development by displaying more flexibility toward Taipei. The positive engagement between the two sides allowed unprecedented stability and full-fledged development across the Strait, including the conclusion of dozens of agreements, an informal diplomatic truce, Taipei's attendance at various international organizations, vigorous economic and social exchanges, multiple official communication mechanisms, and high-ranking political dialogues that culminated in the history-making 2015 Xi–Ma Summit in Singapore.

Second, Washington's adherence to its one-China policy, as well as the cautious and sophisticated handling of the Taiwan issue by the Obama administration, assured Beijing that the US would neither support Taiwan's independence nor seek to use Taiwan as a tool to contain the rise of China. Instead, the US adopted constructive and encouraging postures for the betterment of cross-Strait interaction. At the same time, Beijing reciprocally showed more tolerance and restraint to the development of US–Taiwan substantial relations, despite intensifying competition in the South China Sea and the East China Sea between China and the US.

Third, the US and Taiwan administrations managed their relations prudently according to their respective interests. Taking Washington's concern about disruption of regional security into consideration, Taipei advocated the "Three No's" policy, namely "no independence, no unification and no use of force," and vowed to maintain the status quo across the Strait, which was in the keen interest of the US. Taipei's policy was encouraged by the Obama administration through trade promotion, political endorsement, and diplomatic support, as well as large-scale arms sales amounting to US$14 billion under the arc of a US-defined one-China policy, without worrying these sales would cause the breakup of US–China relations.

One can deduce from the preceding analysis that the realization of positive-sum results among the three parties is necessarily conditional upon a positive cross-Strait relationship, for which the acceptance of the one-China principle by Taipei is the prerequisite. In addition, benign US–China and US–Taiwan relationships are sufficient conditions to ensure peace and stability across the Strait. On the contrary, if the Taiwan administration refuses to accept the one-China principle, just as Chen and Tsai of the DPP did, then Beijing will stop political interaction with Taipei, selectively introduce economic punishment, isolate Taipei internationally, and strengthen military pressure to deter Taipei from pursuing the Taiwan independence agenda publicly or covertly. In response, Taipei will launch a counterattack against Beijing's pressure campaign by mobilizing domestic anti-China and pro-independence forces, and by soliciting international support, especially from the US. At the same time, Beijing will become more vigilant and less tolerant toward the improvement of the US–Taiwan relationship and any US support to Taipei will be interpreted by Beijing as a deliberate challenge to the one-China principle. Consequently, deterioration of the China–US relationship and cross-Strait relationship will inevitably drive Washington and Taipei to enhance US–Taiwan cooperation, which will make Beijing deepen its suspicion further and increase the pressure on both Taipei and Washington in a more confrontational manner. A vicious circle will thus be established.

The most important historical lesson we shall learn from the twists and turns of cross-Strait relations is how to responsibly manage the trilateral relations based on the one-China "position,"[21] which is enshrined by Beijing as an unbreachable red line, defined by Taipei in the Republic of China (ROC) constitution, and accepted by Washington in its one-China policy for decades. Although Beijing will never forswear the use of force to achieve reunification, neither will it ever forget the edification given by Sun Tzu 2,000 years ago that "the leader shall not launch a war because of anger; the general shall not attack the enemy because of sullenness." It is unlikely for Beijing to rashly give up its decade-long peaceful reunification doctrine and undertake "unnecessary" military action against Taipei, unless the latter would antagonize Beijing by pursuing radical de jure independence agenda in the short term or by perpetuating de facto independence in the long term.

Has the alarm already been raised? To some extent, the answer is yes. The relationships between Beijing and Taipei, as well as between Beijing and Washington, have reached the point where an unexpected incidental or accidental "mistake" might spark a nightmarish confrontation. As Joseph Nye warned, inferring from a historical metaphor of World War I, the reckless manipulation of the Taiwan issue amid the deepening great power competition might lead the US and China to "sleepwalk into a conflagration."[22] That said, a military conflict, or a full-scale war for reunification across the Strait involving China and the US, is neither unthinkable nor preordained.[23] Political responsibility and diplomatic wisdom of the three stakeholders are in urgent need to prevent the cross-Strait situation from turning into a precarious race to the bottom in the foreseeable future.

Notes

1 "March 4, 2005: President Hu Jintao Sets Forth Guidelines on Taiwan," *China Daily*, March 4, 2005, https://www.chinadaily.com.cn/china/19thcpcnational congress/2013-03/01/content_29715055.htm.
2 There were unidentified sources around the end of Trump's presidency suggesting that an effort known within the Pentagon as "Fortress Taiwan" was aiming to create a military counterbalance to mainland Chinese forces in the region. See Mike Stone and Patricia Zengerle, "Exclusive: U.S. Pushes Arms Sales Surge to Taiwan, Needling China – sources," *Reuters*, September 6, 2020, https://www.reuters.com/article/us-usa-taiwan-arms-exclusive/exclusive-u-s-pushes

-arms-sales-surge-to-taiwan-needling-china-sources-idUSKBN2671M4. In September 2021, Joseph Wu acclaimed that "Taiwan is a 'sea fortress' blocking China's expansion into the Pacific and is willing to share with other democracies its knowledge of countering Beijing's efforts to undermine it." See Ben Blanchard, "Taiwan Is 'Sea Fortress' against China, Minister Tells U.S. Audience," *Reuters*, September 15, 2021, https://www.reuters.com/world/asia -pacific/taiwan-is-sea-fortress-against-china-minister-tells-us-audience-2021 -09-15. The "hedgehog" or "porcupine" strategy aims at developing Taiwan's military capability in order to withstand pressure or attack from mainland China. See William S. Murray, "Revisiting Taiwan's Defense Strategy," *Naval War College Review* 60, no. 3 (Summer 2008), 2–27. Also see Iain Marlow and Samson Ellis, "Trump Arms Sales to Taiwan Boost Anti-China 'Hedgehog' Strategy," *Bloomberg*, October 27, 2020, updated on October 28, 2020, https:// www.bloomberg.com/news/articles/2020-10-27/trump-arms-sales-to-taiwan -boost-anti-china-hedgehog-strategy. The "Poison Frog Strategy" was first presented in a think-tank report in which the policy recommendations given by the authors is that the United States should strive to turn small, distant off-shore islands like Dongsha into what the players called "poison frogs" to build a credible deterrent against mainland China's military actions, with the essential cooperation of Japan. See Chris Dougherty, Jennie Matuschak, and Ripley Hunter, "The Poison Frog Strategy: Preventing a Chinese Fait Accompli against Taiwanese Islands," Center for a New American Strategy, October 26, 2021, https://www.cnas.org/publications/reports/the-poison-frog-strategy.

3 Rachel Esplin Odell and Eric Heginbotham, "Don't Fall for the Invasion Panic" in "Strait of Emergency? Debating Beijing's Threat to Taiwan," *Foreign Affairs* 100, no. 5 (September–October, 2021), 216–219.

4 Richard Haass and David Sacks, "American Support for Taiwan Must Be Unambiguous," *Foreign Affairs*, September 2, 2020, https://www.foreignaffairs .com/articles/united-states/american-support-taiwan-must-be-unambiguous.

5 Dan Lamothe, "In Taiwan War Game, Few Good Options for U.S. to Deter China," *Washington Post*, October 26, 2021, https://www.washingtonpost.com/ national-security/2021/10/26/us-taiwan-china. The report drafted by the Center for a New American Security is titled "The Poison Frog Strategy," which has been discussed before.

6 Graham Allison, "Could the U.S. Lose a War with China Over Taiwan?," *The National Interest*, October 29, 2021, https://nationalinterest.org/feature/could -us-lose-war-china-over-taiwan-195686.

7 Admiral James Winnefeld, U.S. Navy (Retired), and Michael Morell, "The War That Never Was?" *Proceedings*, August 2020, https://www.usni.org/magazines/ proceedings/2020/august/war-never-was.

8 See Steven Goldstein, "In Defense of Strategic Ambiguity in the Taiwan Strait," National Bureau of Research, October 15, 2021, https://www.nbr.org/publica- tion/in-defense-of-strategic-ambiguity-in-the-taiwan-strait. Also see Richard Bush, "Difficult Choices: Taiwan's Quest for Security and the Good Life," Brookings, April 13, 2021, https://www.brookings.edu/book/difficult-choices.

9 "Hu Jintao: Remarks on the 30th Anniversary of the Mainland's 'Message to Compatriots in Taiwan,'" The Central People's Government of PRC, December 31, 2008, http://www.gov.cn/ldhd/2008-12/31/content_1193074.htm.

10 Li Zhanshu, "Resolutely Oppose the Secession of Taiwan Independence, Firmly Promote the Peaceful Reunification of the Motherland: Address on the 15th

Anniversary of the Implementation of the Anti-Secession Law," Xinhua News Agency, May 29, 2020, http://www.xinhuanet.com/politics/leaders/2020-05/29 /c_1126050630.htm.

11 "President Xi Jinping Had a Virtual Meeting with US President Joe Biden," Ministry of Foreign Affairs of PRC, November 16, 2021, https://www.fmprc .gov.cn/mfa_eng/zxxx_662805/202111/t20211116_10448843.html.

12 Yan Xuetong, "Becoming Strong: The New Chinese Foreign Policy," *Foreign Affairs* 100, no. 4 (July–August 2021), 45.

13 Thomas Christensen, *The China Challenge: Shaping the Choices of a Rising Power* (New York: W.W. Norton & Company, 2015), 295–296.

14 "Xiplomacy: Xi's Remarks Set Direction for Resolving Taiwan Question," Xinhua News Agency, November 20, 2021, http://www.news.cn/english/2021 -11/20/c_1310322653.htm.

15 Philip Wen, "China and Taiwan a 'Family', Says Xi Jinping at Historic Meeting of Leaders," *South China Morning Post*, November 8, 2015, https://www.smh .com.au/world/china-and-taiwan-a-family-says-xi-jinping-at-historic-meeting -of-leaders-20151107-gktf07.html.

16 Wu Xinbo, "On Sino-U.S. Strategic Competition," *World Economics and Politics*, no. 5 (2020), 96–130.

17 The White House, United States, *Interim National Security Strategic Guidance*, March 2021, https://www.whitehouse.gov/wp-content/uploads/2021/03/NSC -1v2.pdf; Ryan Hass, *Stronger: Adapting America's China Strategy in an Age of Competitive Interdependence* (New Haven: Yale University Press, 2021).

18 "Wang Yi Meets with U.S. Secretary of State Antony Blinken," Ministry of Foreign Affairs of PRC, October 31, 2021, https://www.fmprc.gov.cn/mfa_eng /wjb_663304/wjbz_663308/activities_663312/202111/t20211101_10435630 .html.

19 "President Xi Jinping Had a Virtual Meeting with US President Joe Biden," The Ministry of Foreign Affairs of PRC, November 16, 2021, https://www.fmprc .gov.cn/mfa_eng/zxxx_662805/202111/t20211116_10448843.html.

20 Robert D. Blackwill and Philip Zelikow, "The United States, China, and Taiwan: A Strategy to Prevent War," Council on Foreign Relations Special Report, No. 90, February 2021, https://cdn.cfr.org/sites/default/files/report_pdf/csr90_1.pdf.

21 The reason to use one-China "position" here is Beijing always persists on the term of one-China "principle," while Washington insists on the term of one-China "policy."

22 Joseph Nye, "The China Sleepwalking Syndrome," *Project Syndicate*, October 4, 2021.

23 Charles Krulak and Alex Friedman, "The U.S. and China Are Not Destined for War, " China-US Focus, August 24, 2021, https://www.chinausfocus.com/for-eign-policy/the-us-and-china-are-not-destined-for-war.

Index

Page numbers in **bold** denote tables, those in *italic* denote figures.

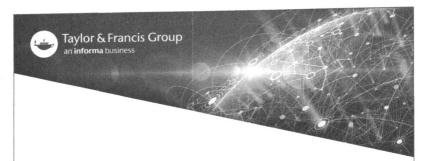

Printed in the United States
by Baker & Taylor Publisher Services